Treasure

Trea

sure
FINDING OUR PAST
RICHARD HOBBS
THE BRITISH MUSEUM PRESS

The Trustees of the British Museum
gratefully acknowledge the generous
support of Anglo American plc and Tarmac.

Message from the Sponsors

Anglo American and Tarmac are committed to respecting the environment and the communities of which we are a part, and to meeting society's future need for materials whilst protecting and preserving treasures from the past.

Both companies are pleased to support the British Museum in this exciting and very special exhibition.

For my Grandmother

First published in 2003 by The British Museum Press
A division of The British Museum Company Ltd
46 Bloomsbury Street, London WC1B 3QQ

A catalogue record for this book is available
from the British Library

ISBN 0 7141 2321 8

Designed by Harry Green
Typeset in Minion and Poetica
Printed in Spain by Grafos S.A. Barcelona

front cover, clockwise from right:
A gold *lunula* necklace from Blessington, County Wicklow, Ireland (fig. 75).

One of the large necklace torcs in the Winchester hoard (fig. 30).

One of the hoards of torcs found at Snettisham, Norfolk (fig. 104).

The helmet from the ship burial found at Sutton Hoo, Suffolk (fig. 3).

back cover:
The Chiddingly boar cap-badge, East Sussex (fig. 63).

Contents

Acknowledgements

Right **Major sites and findspots of treasure mentioned in the text.**

A large number of people have commented on various parts of this book or provided assistance with putting it together. Thanks are due to Richard Abdy, Barry Ager, Angie Bolton, Laura Brockbank, Patrick Clay, Barrie Cook, Nina Crummy, Laura Dance, John Davies, Geoff Egan, Andrew Fitzpatrick, Amy Flint, Hazel Forsyth, David Gaimster, Anna Gannon, David Graham, Harry Green, Peter Guest, Adam Gwilt, Marilyn Hockey, Duncan Hook, Catherine Johns, Kevin Leahy, Michael Lewis, Nigel Meeks, Stuart Needham, Susan La Niece, Tim Pestell, Tony Pilson, Vicki Priest, Mark Redknap, James Robinson, Judy Rudoe, Virginia Smithson, Dora Thornton, Gill Varndell, Lisa Voden Decker, Elizabeth Walker, Leslie Webster, Gareth Williams and Jonathan Williams. Special thanks are due to my colleagues J.D. Hill, Ralph Jackson and Roger Bland at the British Museum, and Edward Besly at the National Museums & Galleries of Wales, for their comments on and contributions to the whole of the text.

This book was written to accompany the temporary exhibition, 'Treasure: Finding our Past'. The exhibition is a collaboration between five different partners which provided venues for the exhibition tour and exhibition content: the British Museum, the National Museums & Galleries of Wales, Norwich Castle Museum & Art Gallery, The Manchester Museum, and Tyne & Wear Museums. The exhibition concept was developed by Richard Hobbs, J.D. Hill and Roger Bland. Additional design and editing of the exhibition at the British Museum was by Teresa Rumble, Jonathan Ould, Paul Goodhead, Richard Dunn, Sam Moorhead and Rebekah Moran. Additional material for the exhibition was provided by the Museum of London, Salisbury and South Wiltshire Museum, North Lincolnshire Museum, Guildford Museum, and Moyse's Hall Museum, Bury St Edmunds.

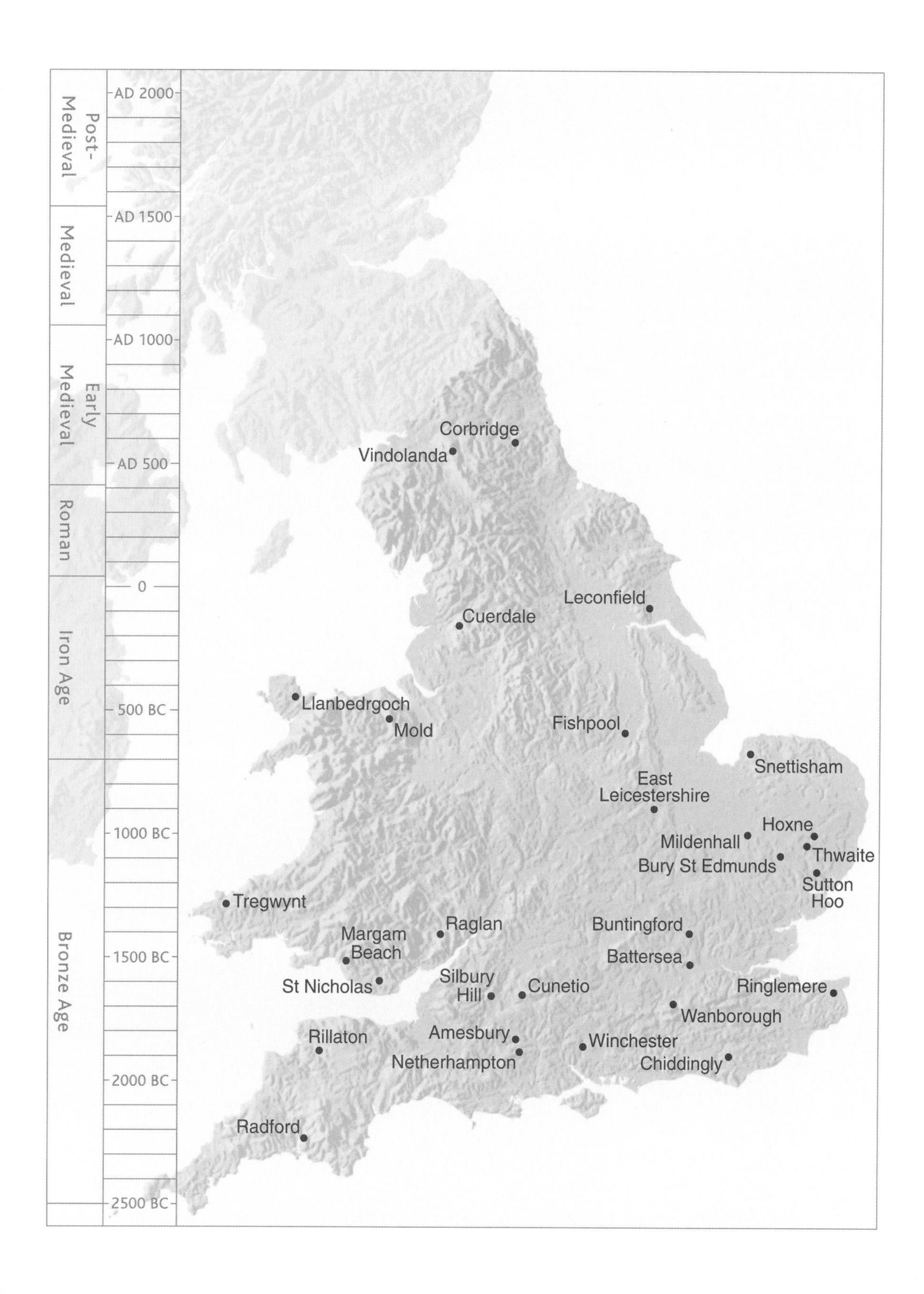

Post-Medieval
Medieval
Early Medieval
Roman
Iron Age
Bronze Age
AD 2000
AD 1500
AD 1000
AD 500
0
500 BC
1000 BC
1500 BC
2000 BC
2500 BC
Corbridge
Vindolanda
Leconfield
Cuerdale
Llanbedrgoch
Mold
Fishpool
Snettisham
East Leicestershire
Hoxne
Mildenhall
Thwaite
Bury St Edmunds
Sutton Hoo
Tregwynt
Raglan
Margam Beach
Buntingford
Battersea
St Nicholas
Silbury Hill
Cunetio
Ringlemere
Wanborough
Rillaton
Amesbury
Winchester
Netherhampton
Chiddingly
Radford

1

What is Treasure?

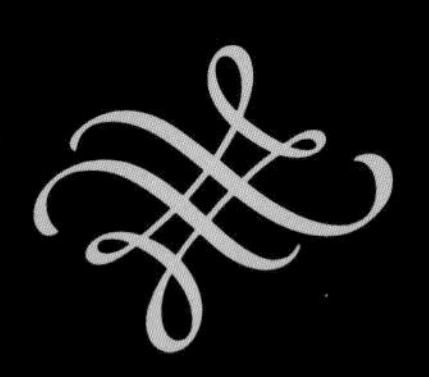

Introduction

Treasure, which comes from the Greek word *thesauros*, has a number of associations in the modern world. 'Buried treasure' and 'sunken treasure' are concepts with which many have grown up in a diverse range of cultures across the globe, from reading *Treasure Island* as children to playing computer games when the discovery of treasure is part of the fun. For most of us, then, the word 'treasure' tends to evoke a combination of precious objects, quest and discovery.

Treasure may also be used in a romantic sense to describe people, for example as a term of endearment in personal relationships. In the wider context it is used to mark out those held in high respect for their achievements: a 'national treasure' is a phrase used to describe those who have made a highly respected contribution to society. This status might be bestowed on someone for their lifetime's achievements, such as Dame Judi Dench for her career as an actress; or for achievements over a much shorter and more intense period, such as some of David Beckham's as Captain of the English football team.

For archaeologists and historians, the word 'treasure' has a rather more specific meaning: it is used as a legal term to define a certain class of archaeological object (see box p. 20). Prior to 1997, an ancient law known as 'Treasure Trove', which dated back to at least the twelfth century AD, meant that any objects of gold and silver for which a legal owner could not be traced were claimed by the Crown. In 1997, this law was superseded by the Treasure Act. Both laws only apply to England, Wales and Northern Ireland; Scotland has a different law (see box p. 13). The rest of this chapter provides a history of Treasure Trove and its eventual reform leading to the present day Treasure Act, and explains how these laws affected the lives of finders of treasure and shaped the treatment of our heritage.

Over the centuries, many different types of people have discovered major treasure finds, including farmers and labourers working the land, homeowners renovating houses, and even people who have claimed special knowledge of treasure through dreams and visions. Most of these discoveries were pure chance; in more recent years, others have deliberately sought to find treasure either by fieldwalking and beachcombing, or by using metal detectors. The major contribution made by all these amateur finders should not be underestimated: in the year 2000, for instance, 276 cases of treasure out of a total of 289 were made by members of the public, rather than archaeologists.[1] This represents over 95 per cent of the total treasure cases reported. Despite this, the role of professionals working in the heritage field should not be overlooked. Professional archaeologists have themselves also made discoveries of treasure finds but, perhaps more importantly, are often charged with the task of following up treasure initially found by amateurs in order that the other essential element to the story – the archaeological context – may be properly established. Chapter 2 looks in more detail at the variety of ways in which treasure, and indeed archaeological objects in general, have been found over the centuries – and how they were subsequently treated. It also describes how these objects found their way into the ground in the first place.

Researching treasure finds, and breathing life into them in order that they take their rightful place in the jigsaw of our past, requires huge dedication on the part of many other professionals. Thus discovery itself is far from being the end of the story. This research is conducted by a range of people, including archaeologists, museum curators, finds specialists, scientists and archaeological conservators. In the wider context, putting finds on display and informing museum and heritage centre visitors about why these objects are important requires equally important input from exhibition designers, museum assistants, education officers and facilitators. Chapters 3 and 4 would not have been possible to write without the contribution of all these individuals.

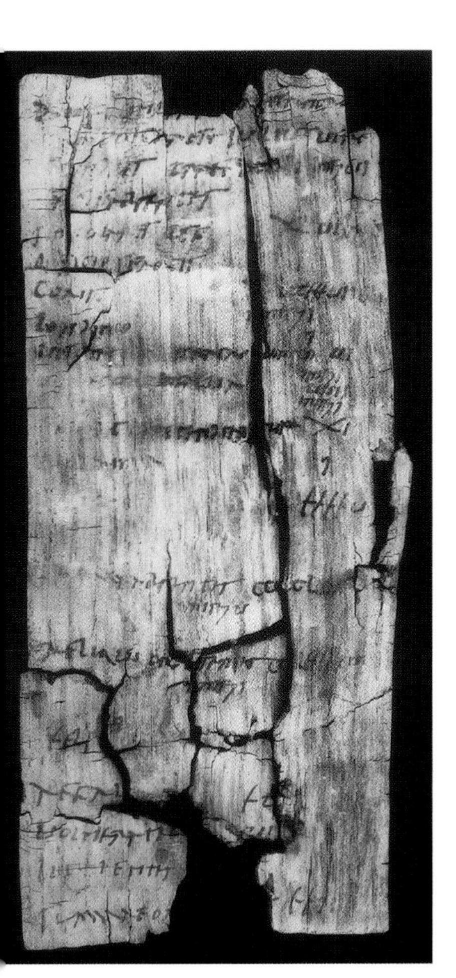

1 A wooden writing tablet from the Roman fort of Vindolanda (modern Chesterholm), Northumberland, dating to *c.* AD 100. Although not 'treasure' in the legal sense, these tablets are of huge importance to understanding the history of the British Isles.

Some finds of treasure are so significant that they have the potential to reshape our understanding of our past completely. Examples of these, from older discoveries which came to us through the law of Treasure Trove, to very recent finds covered by the Treasure Act, are provided in Chapter 3. But, although 'treasure' has a rather narrow definition in legal terms in England and Wales, all archaeological finds should be considered 'treasures'. The smallest sherd of pottery can be as important to understanding our heritage as a magnificent gold buckle which represents the zenith of contemporary craftsmanship: the Vindolanda tablets are a case in point (fig. 1). Some of these less glamorous 'small things forgotten', when looked at as whole sets of objects, can tell equally fascinating stories about the daily lives of their owners, and these are recounted in Chapter 4. Many of these finds have been recorded as a result of the Portable Antiquities Scheme, a voluntary initiative to encourage amateur finders to report all their discoveries (see below, p. 27).

Throughout this book, the role of amateurs and their huge contribution to the discovery of treasure, as both legally defined and in the wider sense of archaeological objects, is highlighted. The word 'treasure' does, however, have a more difficult association for many archaeologists. This is because the word implies a modern financial value for items of immeasurable archaeological worth. And, indeed, treasure finds are by their very nature often of high financial value: they are not only often made of precious gold or silver, but are often rare antiquities. As a result, some people have sought to gain financially from the discovery of treasure and its illicit sale, disregarding the historical importance of the objects. Some of the stories surrounding these unfortunate episodes in the history of treasure discovery are recounted in Chapter 5. These unpalatable incidents teach us that our heritage should never be taken for granted, that our past belongs to everyone, and that we all have equal access rights to it. It is hoped that this book as a whole demonstrates why this is, and should always be, the case.

Treasure Trove: a very ancient law

'Absurd in inception, unjust in operation, and impolitic throughout'[2]

Until it was replaced in 1996, the ancient law of Treasure Trove was one of the oldest laws in the British Isles. The earliest references date back to the twelfth century AD (see box p. 15). Essentially, Treasure Trove provided a means for the Crown to lay claim to any gold or silver which was found in Britain, for which no original owner could be traced. This seems to have derived from the principle that ownerless objects should belong to the King, rather than the finder or landowner. In some cases, the Crown also passed on the rights of Treasure Trove claims to others, such as the Duchies of Cornwall and Lancaster, and ecclesiastical establishments; three or four of these still retain their rights. Local coroner's courts were used to decide whether finds of treasure should be declared Treasure Trove, as they are still today (see p. 24). Over time, Wales took more control over the Treasure Trove process, and Scotland always had a different law covering treasure finds (see box opposite). Finds made in coastal waters or foreshore areas are covered by different legislation (see box p. 29).

Accounts dated to the fourteenth and fifteenth centuries demonstrate that there was a serious lack of consistency in the way finders of such gold and silver were treated. Sometimes they were rewarded for declaring their finds, at others they were treated as little more than common criminals. One such unfortunate finder was a certain Peter White whose case neatly encapsulates the inconsistent way in which the Treasure Trove law was applied. A fourteenth-century parliamentary record runs as follows:

> '14 April, 1400, Westminster
> Peter White of Kensyngton . . . in the 22nd year of Richard II, when labouring on his own business found silver of the coinage of Henry [probably short cross pennies], sometime king of England, amounting to 35 shillings, which sum was mouldy and crumbled like dust, except 5 shillings, and afterwards at the suit of William Scrope, deceased, and other officers of the said late king, he was arrested and imprisoned and still is disturbed and detained under mainprise and has not wherewithal to support himself, the king pardons to him the said 35 shillings.'[3]

Not surprisingly, therefore, many discoveries of gold and silver in the British Isles were not declared as Treasure Trove, and one can only imagine what important archaeological discoveries may have been lost as a result. As Beard and Coates remark:

> 'In the middle of the nineteenth century deliberate and extensive destruction of treasures accidentally found was recorded with painful frequency. The finders, uneducated peasants and labourers for the most part, were naturally not satisfied with the mean sums which the Lords of the Treasury or the similarly responsible officers of Scotland and Ireland saw fit to reward them – purely as an act of grace for their honesty. As a result such finds took the shortest route to the melting pot.'[4]

An early antiquarian account tells of one such case involving a Cornish girl who discovered an ancient gold chain in about 1810. No doubt due to complete ignorance of the importance of the discovery, which nowadays would, ones hopes, be treated with rather more reverence, she apparently decided to use the chain as a whip to drive her cattle. Subsequently the chain was sold by her brother to a local jeweller for the sum of three pounds and probably melted down and recast into new objects.[5]

By the mid-nineteenth century, the authorities started to recognise that, in order to ensure that finds did not end up being sold off and melted down, finders should be properly rewarded for their discoveries if reported correctly. This situation was helped by recognition within the academic world of the importance of these objects to the

Treasure in Wales, Scotland and Northern Ireland

WALES[6]

From the 1880s onwards, the British Museum's administration and pre-emption of Treasure Trove included the occasional case from Wales, although such finds were rare. Meanwhile the foundation of the National Museum of Wales in 1907, with its object 'the complete illustration of the . . . archaeology, art history and special industries of Wales' raised awareness that the acquisition of treasures from Wales by the British Museum was no longer appropriate. As late as 1930, though, twenty-eight of thirty gold nobles (coins) from a fifteenth-century hoard found at Borth, Ceredigion, entered the British Museum's collection, with only two reserved for the National Museum of Wales.

In 1943, lobbying by Professor W.J. Grufydd, MP, persuaded the Chancellor of the Exchequer to concede the right of pre-emption of Treasure Trove in Wales to the National Museum. This was first exercised in 1954 to acquire a find of Bronze Age gold torcs. Even so, it was only in the 1960s that staff of the National Museum of Wales finally took over full responsibility for providing expert evidence to coroners in Wales, while the British Museum continued to value Treasure Troves from Wales until 1977.

Today, arrangements for Treasure in Wales are the same as in England, but administered by staff of the National Museums & Galleries of Wales, using the services of the Treasure Valuation Committee (see p. 24) to set fair rewards for the finders of treasures acquired by Welsh museums.

SCOTLAND

In Scotland, the law of *bona vacantia* was established at a similar date to the common law of Treasure Trove and still applies today. *Bona vacantia* literally means 'ownerless items'. This means that if any artefacts are discovered on Scottish soil, irrespective of why they are there and of what material they are made, the Crown has the right to claim them. In a similar manner to Treasure Trove, this law was initially used to swell the royal coffers, but since the nineteenth century has been used to benefit Scottish archaeology. The law means that in principle all archaeological discoveries are protected.

NORTHERN IRELAND[7]

In Northern Ireland, the old common law of Treasure Trove applied until 1996 when the Treasure Act came into effect. However, there is also a statutory duty to report all finds of archaeological objects, as well as legal controls over archaeological excavations, neither of which exists in England or Wales. The 1995 Historic Monuments and Archaeological Objects (Northern Ireland) Order includes a statutory requirement for the finder of any archaeological object to report the circumstances of its discovery and the nature of the object within fourteen days. The find should be reported to the Ulster Museum, the police or the Department of the Environment for Northern Ireland, who may retain it for up to three months. In addition, the Order makes it an offence to excavate any land while searching for archaeological objects without a licence. The Order also contains provisions for archaeological objects found on scheduled monuments.

2 The Corbridge Lanx, fourth century AD, found in Northumberland in 1735. The lanx, a silver 'picture plate', depicts a temple of Apollo and is one of the earliest known cases of Treasure Trove.

understanding of the early history of the British Isles. The antiquarian Sir John Evans (1823–1908), for example, recognised the vital link between knowing where Celtic coins had been discovered and the distribution of Iron Age British tribal groupings.[8] In addition, the establishment of the British Museum in 1753 and the emergence of a network of local museums meant that important discoveries of treasure had more chance of being preserved. The British Museum began to act as a repository for finds which had come through the Treasure Trove process, effectively holding them on behalf of the Crown and the nation. Although archival records for the eighteenth and nineteenth centuries are very sketchy, these finds included a small set of Viking silver from the Isle of Man, and some Anglo-Saxon gold and silver from Warwickshire, both acquired as Treasure Trove by the British Museum in the 1870s. Other finds were preserved as the result of the tenacity of Treasure Trove franchise holders. A good example is the Corbridge Lanx (fig. 2), a Roman silver platter found by a nine-year-old girl on the banks of the river Tyne in 1735. The lanx was sold to a local goldsmith but claimed by the Treasure Trove franchise holder, the seventh Duke of Somerset – only after he had issued an injunction preventing the goldsmith from 'alienating, defacing or melting it down'. The Duke successfully acquired the object, where it was kept as part of the family's holdings until loaned to and eventually acquired by the British Museum in the 1990s.[9]

The Government was also beginning to recognise that, without rewarding finders, very little Treasure Trove material was being declared. Thus in 1858, Lord Talbot de Malahide tried and failed to introduce a Private Members Bill to change the law.[10] But in 1886, the Treasury finally established the principle of paying rewards to finders, and the British Museum was also given the task of valuing Treasure Trove finds and deciding where they should be placed – either in the national collection itself or a suitable local museum.

Treasure Trove and Sutton Hoo

As we have seen, by the twentieth century Treasure Trove could result in the preservation of important antiquities from Britain. However, it was still a very ancient law and offered little protection to most archaeological discoveries. This became clear in 1939 when excavations at Sutton Hoo in Suffolk led to a spectacular discovery.[11] A group of circular burial mounds had been known at the site for many years, and a number had been robbed in the past. But miraculously, when the largest of these

The earliest references to Treasure Trove

Although there are mentions of Treasure Trove dating to the time of Henry I (AD 1100–35) and Edward the Confessor (AD 1042–66), the most comprehensive passages relating to Treasure Trove can be found in a manuscript of Henry de Bracton, dated to about AD 1250.[12] The following passage neatly encapsulates the law; it is interesting to note that both land and sea finds were covered:

'Things which are regarded as derelict are also said to be no one's property. Things such as treasure are said to belong to no one by reason of lapse of time. Also where the owner of the thing does not appear, as with wreck of the sea. Also in the case of things which are regarded as waif, as cattle, where the owner does not appear; and things which formerly belong to the finder by natural law now become the property of the sovereign by the law of nations.'

Further on, specific reference is made to precious metals:

'There is among other things a serious act of presumption against the King, his dignity, and Crown, which indeed is as it were a crime of theft, to wit the fraudulent concealment of treasure trove. So that if any one shall have been accused of having found treasure, to wit silver or gold or other kind of metal . . .'

There are also clear references to the involvement of coroners, even at this early stage in British legal history:

'As to procedure, speaking of the coroners: it is their office, as soon as they have a mandate from the bailiff of our lord the King or from the good men of that neighbourhood, to visit the slain or wounded or drowned or suddenly dead, and go to houses broken into and the place where treasure is said to be found. . . . First they ought to inquire of those who are accused thereof, and whether any one be found seised thereof, or if there be presumption against any one that he has found treasure, because he carries himself more abundantly in feeding and more richly in dress. . . . And if such be found, he ought to be attached by four or six or more securities if they can be found.'

3 The helmet from the ship burial found at Sutton Hoo, Suffolk, dating to the early seventh century AD. The site of Sutton Hoo illustrated the inadequacies of the Treasure Trove law for protecting archaeological material of national importance.

mounds was opened, a magnificent ship burial was discovered intact and largely undisturbed. The finds, which were of remarkable wealth and richness, included the famous helmet and face mask (fig. 3), Byzantine silver vessels, beautiful gold and garnet belt-fittings and shoulder clasps (fig. 4), and superb examples of arms and armour. The burial was dated to the early part of the seventh century AD, and may have belonged to King Raedwald who died in AD 624/5. The discovery was of huge importance for the understanding of a period of British history for which archaeological evidence is relatively poor.

Although the Sutton Hoo burial clearly contained gold and silver, it was not strictly Treasure Trove in the legal sense. One of the anomalies of the Treasure Trove law was that in order to qualify, it had to be demonstrated that the original owners of the treasure had intended to recover their find. In such cases, the Crown justified laying claim to such finds, as the failure to recover the buried objects had effectively left them ownerless.

The ship burial at Sutton Hoo, however, was an obvious case of burial where there had never been the intention to recover. These objects had been placed with the remains of an important person in ancient society, with the wish that they should be with him for eternity. Therefore at a coroner's inquest in 1939, it was decided that the burial and all its contents did not qualify as Treasure Trove. The Crown could have challenged this ruling because, since the thirteenth century, treasure from barrows was the property of the King who was also able to grant licences to excavate such sites. But such a challenge never became necessary: soon after the inquest ended, the landowner, Mrs Edith Pretty, who had been awarded the treasure, generously gave it to the nation. This was a fortunate outcome as all the finds were preserved and many are now on permanent display at the British Museum; but it could have been very different, as Treasure Trove had failed to protect an archaeological discovery that was key for understanding the history of the British Isles.

4 A gold belt buckle from Sutton Hoo, Suffolk, early seventh century AD.

The dawn of the metal detector

If Sutton Hoo was the first indication of the inadequacies of the Treasure Trove law, then the arrival of the metal detector really threw this into sharp focus. In the 1970s, metal detecting devices became widely available and relatively cheap to buy. Such machines, which had developed from mine detectors used to clear landmines by the military, had been used occasionally by archaeologists in the post-war period when they wanted to locate the findspots of important metalwork. For instance, in 1946 the archaeologists Fowler and Lethbridge used heavy and cumbersome metal detecting devices to search for more pieces from the Mildenhall treasure (see p. 76 and fig. 47).

The new lighter and affordable machines quickly led to the creation of a new hobby. Initially, most metal detectors were purchased by people who wanted to search beaches and other coastal areas for money and jewellery lost in recent times, which soon led to their nickname of 'treasure hunters'. Users then moved from beaches on to country footpaths and farmers' fields, and started to find metal objects which were not necessarily recent losses. Unfortunately, a minority of metal detector users took to searching known archaeological sites, often at night, which earned them the nickname of 'nighthawks'. To the disgust of many archaeologists and responsible detectorists, their activities were even glamorised in a television documentary.

By the 1980s, metal detecting was one of the fastest growing hobbies in the UK, with one report estimating that as many as 30,000 people were regular participants.[13] Detectorists, in order to gain access to more land, started to make arrangements with local farmers and landowners to allow them to pursue their hobby. A national body was set up to represent their interests in the UK, and in 1995 this split into the National Council for Metal Detecting (NCMD) and the Federation of Independent Detectorists (FID). Both bodies are still operating today and provide their members with advice and guidance on the safe and responsible pursuit of their hobby (see p. 150). They also have regular contact with Government over matters which affect their members. Both organisations contributed to the formulation of the Treasure Act (1996), and expressed their views on how the Portable Antiquities Scheme (see below, p. 27) should operate.

The popularity of metal detecting, particularly during the 1980s, was not welcomed by many archaeologists working in Britain. Finders were often perceived as being nothing more than 'treasure hunters' seeking to destroy and sell our heritage, and some archaeologists took every possible opportunity to tell farmers not to allow metal detectorists on to their land. The destruction of high profile sites such as the Roman temple at Wanborough in Surrey (see p. 142) even led to calls for the hobby to be banned. It is estimated that as many as 20,000 artefacts could have been lost during the looting of Wanborough, as hordes of treasure hunters from all over the country dug massive holes into the site in their quest for riches (see fig. 107). For their part, metal detectorists grew increasingly resentful of archaeologists, whom they saw as being high-handed and obstructive. Many felt that archaeologists behaved as if they were the only people who had the right to excavate archaeological material. There was also an obvious conflict of interests because metal detectorists kept many of their finds in their own homes, whilst most finds excavated by archaeologists were passed to local museums where they were accessible to all.

There were some archaeologists, however, who actively embraced what detecting could offer in the pursuit of understanding our past. In Norfolk, the late Tony Gregory recognised the potential of metal detectors and the skill of their users – if they were honest and responsible – as a valuable archaeological tool. He therefore forged strong relationships with local detector groups, attending their meetings and recording their finds. Whilst excavating the Iron Age and Roman site of Fison Way, Thetford, Gregory used local detectorists during survey and excavation work.[14] He realised that it was far better to try to work with them than actively to attempt to ban their activities. For their part, the detectorists with whom Gregory liaised were able to see at first hand how archaeological sites worked, understand the importance of properly recording finds, and feel valued as members of an archaeological team. But Gregory also pursued the 'nighthawks' who illegally raided archaeological sites. Thanks to good links forged with the local police, a number of prosecutions were made. This progressive approach was taken up by others working in Britain's many museums, who would often spend their leisure time visiting metal detector clubs to encourage good finders and gather information about material not being reported. These small pockets of positive relations set the scene for what was to come (fig. 5).

5 A controlled metal detecting survey in the parish of Wyre Piddle, Worcestershire, organised by Angie Bolton of the Portable Antiquities Scheme. Metal detecting is a hugely popular hobby in Britain.

The Treasure Act: a new beginning

The popularity of metal detecting in the last decades of the twentieth century unsurprisingly led to an increase in the number of Treasure Trove cases. As detectorists spread out across the ploughed fields of England and Wales, they would occasionally make important discoveries which in some cases were extremely large, for instance the Cunetio hoard (see p. 69). Curators at the British Museum and the National Museum of Wales found themselves spending greater proportions of their time dealing with Treasure Trove finds, particularly coin hoards of the Iron Age, Roman and medieval periods.

As a result of the problems with Treasure Trove, pressure began to build within the archaeological community to reform the law. Around 1990, the Surrey Archaeological Society, in response to the failure of the prosecutions of those caught looting at Wanborough (see p. 142), began to work on a new bill to reform the law. They secured

The Treasure law today

'Treasure' is now defined as follows:

- any object more than 300 years old when found which is made of more than 10 per cent gold or silver;
- at least two gold or silver coins from the same find, or ten or more of base metal (copper-alloy or tin);
- more than two objects of prehistoric metalwork from the same find with less than 10 per cent gold or silver;
- any objects found in association with treasure, for example, human bones found in a grave with gold or silver items, or the pottery container of a coin hoard.

a doughty champion, the late Lord Perth, and the support of the British Museum. Roger Bland, then a curator in the Department of Coins and Medals at the British Museum, was seconded by the Government to work on the bill. A huge number of interested parties from archaeologists and museum curators to the metal detectorists themselves were approached for their views, and the new Treasure Act finally passed through parliament in 1996. It came into force a year later.

The Treasure Act was a major improvement on the old law of Treasure Trove. It defined for the first time exactly what constituted treasure (see box above), and ensured that material found in association with treasure finds also qualified – for example, the pottery container of a silver coin hoard (fig. 6). But, most importantly, it finally abolished the principle that there had to be an intention on the part of the depositor to recover treasure finds. As was shown by cases such as Sutton Hoo, this had been a major problem presented by the old common law of Treasure Trove.

The Treasure Act has proved to be an enormous success. Since it was introduced, the number of treasure finds which have been reported has increased twelve-fold, with over 300 treasure cases in 2002 alone. More importantly, the types of find which are now seen have greatly expanded. Medieval rings, Tudor dress-fittings and whole grave groups such as the Amesbury archer (see pp. 53, 123 and 127), are just a few examples of the new categories of object which can now be acquired by museums. There have also been some spectacular successes with regard to the discovery and subsequent excavation of major archaeological sites. Two examples are the Iron Age gold jewellery from Winchester, Hampshire (see p. 59), and the Bronze Age gold cup from Ringlemere, Kent (see p. 55).

6 The Field Baulk hoard of Iron Age silver coins of the early first century AD, found in Cambridgeshire in 1982. Under the new Treasure law, the pottery container for the hoard would qualify as treasure along with the coins.

The Act will also be reviewed on a regular basis to ensure that it is working well. The first of

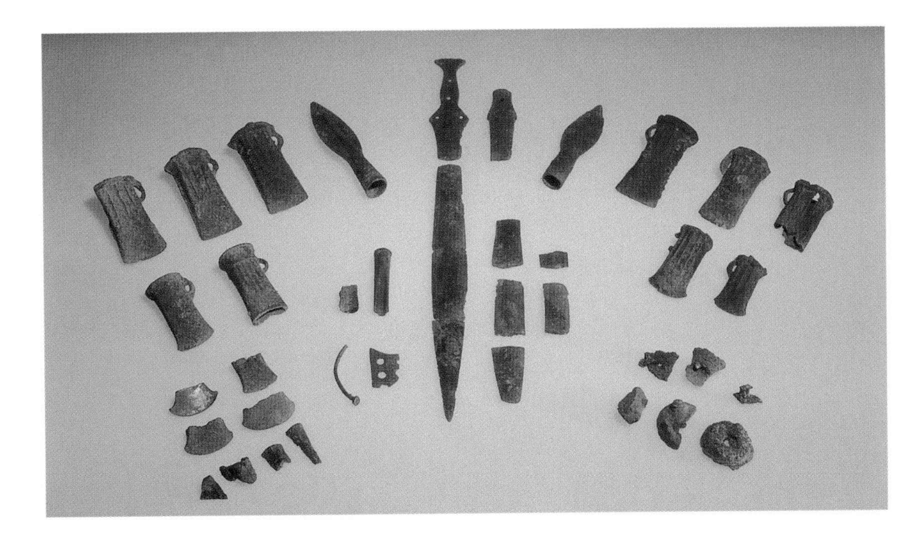

7 Metalwork hoard from St Nicholas, Glamorgan, Wales, dating to the late Bronze Age. This hoard is an example of a prehistoric base metal deposit, which since 2002 also qualify as Treasure if discovered in England, Wales or Northern Ireland.

these reviews took place in 2002 and, as a result, it was decided that hoards of prehistoric metalwork, such as the St Nicholas hoard from the Vale of Glamorgan in Wales (fig. 7), not originally covered by the Act, would in future also count as treasure. This means that another important type of archaeological material has legal protection.

A year in the life of a treasure find

So what actually happens to treasure when it is discovered? The next section follows one find through from discovery to acquisition by a museum.

The finder

This story begins with the finding of a cross, about 8 cm in length, in a ploughed field near the village of Thwaite in Suffolk, in the spring of 1999 (fig. 8). The finders were local metal detector users, Mike Seager and Andy Slinn, both members of the Ipswich and District Metal Detecting Club. The club meets monthly, and is often visited by the Finds Liaison Officer, part of the Portable Antiquities Scheme (see p. 27) based at Suffolk County Council. The Finds Liaison Officer at the time, Gabor Thomas, collected the cross from the club and took it back to his office for examination and recording. This was a normal part of Gabor's work with the Portable Antiquities Scheme – a number of metal detecting clubs have an agreement with the scheme's officers that finds can be taken away from meetings for recording. Afterwards finds are returned to members, usually at the next meeting.

The finds liaison officer

Back at the offices of Suffolk County Council, the find was then properly examined for the first time. It was clear that there was an engraving on the cross in the form of a figure, which seemed likely to be that of Christ. This meant that it was probably of medieval date – figures of Christ do not usually appear on artefacts until this period.

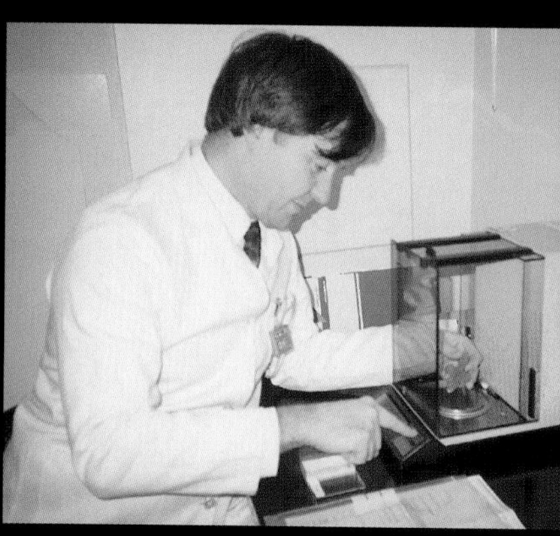

8 The Thwaite cross, found during metal detecting in Suffolk in early 1999.

9 James Robinson, curator of medieval antiquities at the British Museum, examining the Thwaite cross.

10 British Museum scientist, Duncan Hook, examining the Thwaite cross. Scientific work is a vital part of the treasure process and finds research.

So already quite a lot could be deduced just from a relatively brief examination of the object – finds specialists are often able quickly to ascertain what most objects are and to what period they date. However, at this stage, the function and precise date of the cross were unclear, so it was decided to seek a second opinion. It was also uncertain of what metal it was made. The cross was a dull brown colour which implied that it was made of copper-alloy, but only scientific analysis would clarify this. For all these reasons, the cross was passed to the British Museum for further investigation. If the find had been discovered in Wales, it would have been passed on to the National Museum in Cardiff instead.

The curator

Once at the British Museum, the cross was passed to James Robinson, an expert on medieval objects (fig. 9). Details of the cross were also recorded with Lisa Voden Decker, the Treasure Registrar, as it might be treasure. James was able to add to Gabor Thomas's initial findings – he confirmed that the cross was medieval in date, but, more importantly, he was able to work out its function. It was the upper part of a reliquary which would have originally contained a religious relic. The lower half of the reliquary was missing, as well as the relic itself. The surviving part would have been attached to the bottom half with a hinge and a clasp. The cross also had a suspension loop at the top, so could have been worn around the neck. Such items are very rare finds.

A closer examination of the engraving confirmed that it showed Christ on the cross. Christ was wearing a knee-length tunic and had a halo. Above the figure was the Hand of God. James was also able to establish that the cross was probably made in Scandinavia as it compared closely with examples from Denmark in the National Museum in Copenhagen. These comparable examples also narrowed down the date of the cross more closely to the late eleventh or twelfth centuries AD (it was not possible to be much more precise). Surviving complete examples also suggest that the missing half may have been engraved with the figure of the Virgin Mary. This meant that the cross probably came into Britain before or soon after the Norman Conquest in AD 1066, undoubtedly the most well-known date in British history. The other question which still had to be answered, however, was of what material the cross was made.

The scientist

The British Museum employs scientists alongside artefact experts such as James Robinson, and one of their main jobs is to establish what objects are made of and how they were constructed. So in this case, James sent the cross over to Duncan Hook in the Department of Conservation, Science and Documentation for examination (fig. 10). Duncan used a technique called X-ray fluorescence (XRF) to examine the metal content of the cross. This involves aiming an X-ray beam at the surface of the object; the X-rays interact with the metal and produce other, distinctive (fluorescent) X-rays from which the proportions of different metal components can be calculated. This method is frequently used because it is non-destructive so samples do not have to be removed from objects for it to work.

Somewhat surprisingly, it transpired that the cross was made of about 53 per cent silver – so even though it looked rather dull in colour, it was in fact made mostly of precious metal. In addition, another scientist, Susan La Niece, was able to look at the decoration on the cross and establish that originally the cross was also gilded, slight traces of which remained, so it would once have been much shinier. There were also traces of niello in the engravings of Christ. Niello, a black silver paste, was popular in both Roman and medieval times as a way of picking out the detail of engraved decoration.

The Department's role is extremely important to the treasure process, because for finds to qualify as treasure, they need to contain at least 10 per cent gold or silver (see box p. 20). At 53 per cent, the cross clearly did, which meant that it fulfilled all the requirements for treasure: it was more than 300 years old and made of more than 10 per cent precious metal, and was found on English soil.

The cross was then photographed, and James and Duncan wrote reports for the coroner. James also had to decide if he wished the British Museum to acquire it; normally he discusses this issue with the local museums who might also want to add it to their collections. In this case, it was agreed that the British Museum would try to add it to its holdings because the cross was quite rare and would thus form an important part of the national collections. By no means all treasure cases are acquired by the British Museum – most are retained by regional museums. But museums generally acquire only a small proportion of treasure finds – the majority of treasure objects are returned to their finders.

The coroner

The next stage was the coroner's inquest. Coroners have been part of the treasure process since the old days of Treasure Trove (see box p. 15). Their role is to provide an independent means by which treasure finds can be assessed to ensure that everyone is treated fairly and that the objects in question meet the legal requirements of treasure. So an inquest was held on 11 November 1999 at Southwold, Suffolk, at the court of the coroner for the Lowestoft district, where the find was discovered. The find was declared treasure, so it now needed to be valued.

The Treasure Valuation Committee

The cross had to be valued by the Treasure Valuation Committee (TVC) so that a reward could be made to the finder (fig. 11). The TVC meets about six times a year and consists of experts drawn from the antiquities trade, museums and the National Council for Metal Detecting (NCMD). However, before the cross could be considered by the TVC, it was valued by two independent antiquities experts, based at major London auction houses. It was then placed on the agenda for the next TVC meeting, held on 14 January 2000, and the experts' valuations were provided to the members of the committee.

At the meeting, it was decided that the cross should be valued at £1,500. Decisions about the value of individual treasure finds are based upon an estimate of the full price they are likely to fetch at auction, which will depend upon the object's rarity, historical or archaeological importance, collectability, and its condition. In this case, the valuation was accepted by the finder, the landowner and the Museum, although

11 The Treasure Valuation Committee (TVC) discussing the valuation of treasure finds. The Committee's role is essential for deciding fair rewards for the finders of treasure.

each has the right to appeal. The British Museum was then able to acquire the cross. The Museum has a small budget to buy new objects, but often has to seek help from other sources including the British Museum Friends and the National Art Collections Fund. In this case, the money was found from the Museum's own budget and the finders were paid. Rewards for treasure are usually split 50/50 between the finder and the landowner. The cross is now part of the British Museum's collections and thus a guaranteed part of the nation's heritage.

The conservator

The story of the cross does not quite end there. It was rather dirty after being in the ground for over 1,000 years, so it was gently cleaned by the conservation department. Its storage requirements were also assessed. The way in which objects are stored depends upon the material they are made of, and special materials are used to ensure that objects are properly supported. If not stored correctly, they can easily deteriorate. In this case, the cross needed to be safe from physical damage, so it was placed in a special inert foam cut-out; and to prevent it from corroding, it was kept in a special environment with low levels of moisture in the air. Objects on display are treated in exactly the same way, with the conservation department ensuring that they are free from dust, that humidity levels are appropriate, and that lighting is suitable.

The exhibition team

The cross will be displayed as part of the 'Treasure' exhibition which opens at the British Museum in November 2003.[15] Many people are involved in bringing this exhibition together. In the case of the Thwaite cross, the designers will decide how it is best displayed and, together with the curators, will compose the panel text. Museum assistants and specialists will have to make a special mount tailored to suit the cross in its display case and, as the exhibition is travelling to different venues, the cross will have to be packaged up and taken to the different exhibition partners.

THE LEGACY OF THE THWAITE CROSS

With all archaeological finds, not just the Thwaite cross, the story never comes to an end. At the time of publication, the cross is on display as part of a temporary exhibition, but in future it might be selected for permanent display at the British Museum. In addition, although a short report has appeared which explains what it is and why it is important,[16] this does not tell the whole story. There are still many questions to be answered: to whom did it belong? Where and how exactly was it made? How did it end up in Suffolk? We and future generations might be able to answer these questions by conducting more research and coming up with new approaches and ideas. Other similar finds might be discovered which change our view of it completely. There is even a small chance that the rest of the reliquary may be discovered. The results of this work will be published in books or articles, in both printed form and relatively new media such as the Internet. But the most important point is that the Thwaite cross has been preserved which means that its future as a tiny piece of the jigsaw of our past is assured.

12 Around 11,000 metal objects collected by metal detectorist Mr Walter Carlile in one parish of Lincolnshire over the course of two decades. Though large, the assemblage represents only a fraction of the finds recovered by amateurs annually in Britain. The collection was acquired in its entirety by North Lincolnshire Museum.

Showing their metal: the Portable Antiquities Scheme

1997 was an important year for British archaeology, not just because of the new Treasure Act, but also because of the introduction of the Portable Antiquities Scheme. When the new Act was being formulated, it was recognised that, although much more treasure material would now be reported, many more objects important to our heritage would not. Any metal detectorist will tell you that finds of gold, silver, coins or metalwork hoards are few and far between – on an average day, old bits of farm machinery and Victorian shoe buckles are more likely to be recovered than a Roman coin hoard. Nevertheless, all the non-treasure finds are potentially of huge importance to Britain's history. By recording these finds, we can learn more about where people were living, what they were wearing, with whom they were trading, and how all these things changed over time. The volume of such material is huge: hundreds of thousands of objects are recovered every year in England and Wales by an estimated 5,000 to 10,000 metal detector users. One metal detectorist discovered an astonishing 11,000 objects in just one parish in Lincolnshire over the course of two decades (fig. 12).

The Portable Antiquities Scheme was therefore set up to encourage finders to report all their discoveries, both metal and other. The Scheme, which originally started as a pilot project, has been a huge success. Finders do not have to report finds as the project is voluntary, but are encouraged to do so by regionally based Finds Liaison Officers, who link up with detectorists in their local area. This often means evenings spent in the smoky backrooms of pubs, sifting through all the finds of a local metal detecting club, recording and identifying all sorts of objects (fig. 13). Detectorists do not just find metalwork, they also often pick up prehistoric flints and pottery of all periods, and recording this material allows Finds Liaison Officers to build up a picture of the archaeology of their local area. Officers also hold regular finds identification days (or 'finds surgeries'), usually in

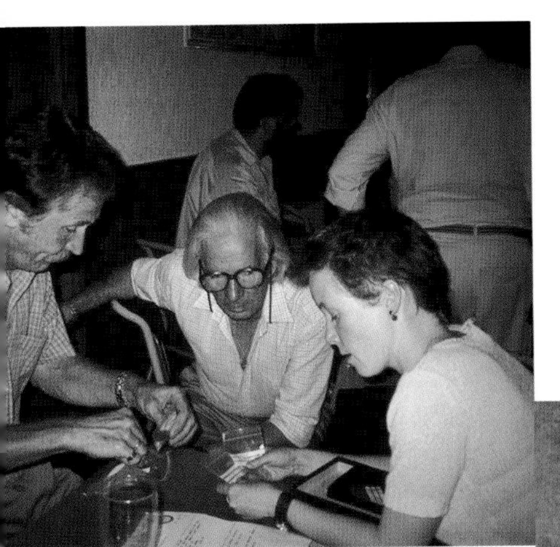

13 *Above* Angie Bolton, Finds Liaison Officer in the West Midlands (right), examining finds at the Tamworth Metal Detecting Club.

14 Sally Worrell, Finds Liaison Officer in Hampshire (second from left), recording finds made by the public at English Heritage's 'Archaeology Day' held annually at Portchester Castle.

conjunction with their local museum, and this is another way in which the public are able to report their discoveries (fig. 14). In addition, the Finds Liaison Officers educate finders as to why recording findspots for their discoveries is so important, and also provide advice on the Treasure Act and issues such as conservation and storage.

Where next for treasure and portable antiquities?

In 2003, the Portable Antiquities Scheme was expanded to cover the whole of England and Wales, after a successful bid to the Heritage Lottery Fund. This will mean that throughout these two countries, amateur finders will be encouraged to volunteer their finds for recording, and the public will be better informed about the importance of preserving and recording our heritage for the future. In addition, the expansion of the Scheme will certainly lead to a greater number of treasure cases being processed: many objects will be able to be acquired by local and national museums, which can only help to improve our knowledge of the past and provide future generations with material to research and enjoy.

Despite these very positive developments, there are still many problems which need to be resolved. At a local level, museums and archaeological services are constantly battling against declining budgets and grant cuts. The acuteness of the problem has been recognised by the government's advisory body for museums (Resource[17]), and it is hoped that the recommendation for greater investment in heritage at a local level will be realised. In addition, many archaeological finds still go unreported, although the exact scale of the problem is extremely hard to judge. The Salisbury hoard is a case in point, and is a sad example of the way in which important discoveries can be broken up and sold to antiquities dealers (see p. 144). In fact, there are moves towards giving better protection to antiquities found in Britain, particularly as the UK government has recently signed the 1970 UNESCO Convention, set up to control the trade in art and antiquities.[18] A bill has also been introduced into Parliament to create a new offence of dealing in cultural objects which have been illegally excavated (see p. 148).

Conclusion

This chapter has provided important background to the legal framework in which treasure finds have been discovered and reported over the centuries. The next chapter looks at how treasure, and other archaeological material, ended up in the ground in the first place. The second part shows how these objects were then discovered through the actions of people in modern times, sometimes by pure chance, sometimes by active searching, and on occasion as the result of dreams and visions.

15 Spanish coin talers and navig dividers, all four Margam Beach, Talbot, south Wa probably from th of the *Ann Franc* King's Lynn, wre December 1583.

Wreck and foreshore

Britain's coastline has been one of the most hazardous places in the world for ships since man first began to navigate the seas. Frequent storms and unpredictable currents, allied with primitive methods of navigation, have resulted in many thousands of vessels of all shapes and sizes being sunk.

Because of the huge number of sunken vessels around the British coastline, the UK is a very popular location for recreational diving: there are an estimated 70,000 divers, many of whom look for the remains of ships. Although most of these divers are content simply to observe, some recover artefacts and material from these wreck sites, not unlike metal detectorists who scour farmland for archaeological finds (fig. 15). Some divers are even professional salvagers of sunken wrecks. Fishermen also sometimes bring up material from the seabed in their fishing nets. In addition, many parts of the British coastline are happy hunting grounds for beachcombers who are sometimes able to locate material which has been washed up on the shore.

Wreck and foreshore finds are protected by UK laws in a similar manner to treasure. The Merchant Shipping Act (1995) stipulates that all wreck material recovered from UK territorial waters, or brought within UK territorial waters, must be reported to the Receiver of Wreck, an official of the Maritime and Coastguard Agency (MCA). The Receiver of Wreck must establish if an owner for the material can be traced, and the opportunity is then given to the owner to salvage their vessel. In the case of archaeological finds, material might instead be offered to a local museum, and the finder would receive a reward just as with finds of treasure (see p. 24).

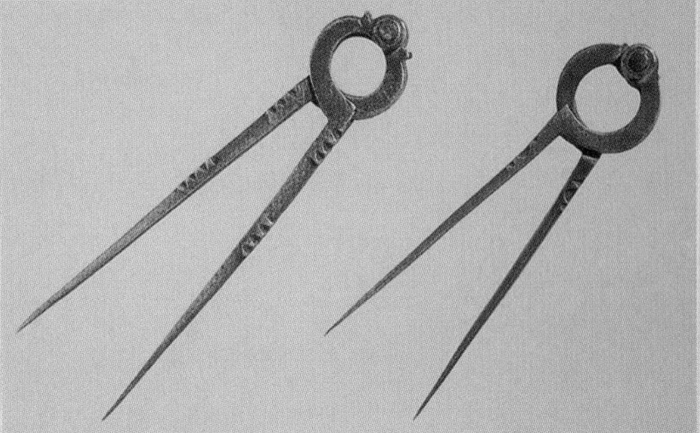

Definitions of wreck

FLOTSAM – goods lost from a ship which remain afloat
JETSAM – goods cast overboard to lighten a vessel in danger
LAGAN – goods buoyed and cast overboard for later recovery
DERELICT – any part of a vessel or its cargo which has been abandoned or deserted at sea

Many divers have been unaware of the law regarding wreck, or have chosen to ignore it in the past. For this reason, in the early part of 2001, the Receiver of Wreck set up a Wreck Amnesty, which allowed finds of wreck to be reported without any legal action taken against finders for non-reporting. The Amnesty proved a huge success, with 4,600 reports of wreck finds submitted to the Receiver. The final report of the Wreck Amnesty can be obtained from the MCA.[19]

2

Finding the Past

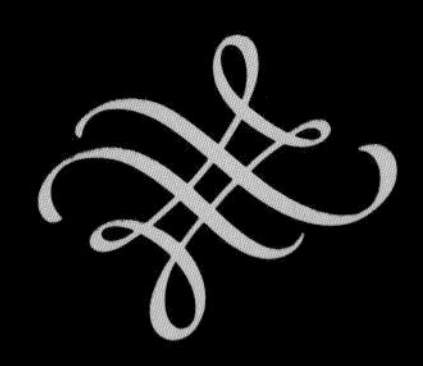

Introduction

At the end of the last chapter, the popularity of metal detecting in Britain as a hobby was highlighted. Metal detecting is one way in which discoveries of archaeological material are made, but it is far from being the only method, and was almost unheard of until the 1970s. Prior to this, for many hundreds of years, chance discoveries of treasure and other archaeological finds were quite common. This chapter looks at the different ways in which archaeological objects – often termed portable antiquities – have been discovered.

This chapter also looks at the action that people have taken after making their discoveries, which has a huge effect on what we are able to understand about a particular find, and is an essential element in telling the story of different discoveries. The 'archaeological context' for a find – knowing exactly where it came from and how it ended up in the ground – is easily as important as the find itself. This is so often overlooked, particularly in the case of 'glamorous' treasure objects when the general public often thinks that the financial worth of the object is *all* that matters. To properly understand finds, we have to know their context – it would not be too contentious to say that without this information finds are rendered virtually worthless.

But before any of these issues can be examined, it is necessary to take one step back. How did 'things' end up in the ground in the first place? The way in which archaeological sites form is a whole subject in its own right, and there is not room to explore it here. Suffice to say that such sites, including findspots of treasure, produce two main categories of evidence: features, such as walls, pits, defences and so on, and the objects found within these features. Archaeological objects can be both natural, such as animal bone; or man-made objects – artefacts – such as coins.

Some finds discussed in this book come from sites where archaeological features are easily distinguished. Examples are items found in graves, such as the burial of the Amesbury archer (see p. 53). In this case the objects consisted of both natural items such as human bone, and artefacts such as the archer's flint arrowheads. The archaeological features were the edges of the grave in which the body and the other objects had been placed, and it was these features that provided the archaeological context for these particular finds.

But many finds in this book do not have associated features, although they often do have an archaeological context. For example, when the findspot of the Iron Age jewellery from Winchester (see p. 59) was excavated, no archaeological features were discovered. But it nonetheless had a context because the lack of recognisable features – for example a grave – was a context in its own right. However, other discoveries in this book have no known archaeological features and thus no context at all. This is usually because knowledge of their exact findspot has been lost, making investigation impossible. Once again, this has an effect on the stories we can tell about particular finds.

How precious objects became buried

Archaeological objects could have ended up in the ground in a number of ways. Some were simply discarded or abandoned when they were seen as no longer having any useful purpose to their owners, for example broken pottery. There are essentially two ways in which other types of personal possession, including items made of precious materials, could have ended up in the ground (which does not necessarily mean dry land). The first is accidental – the unplanned loss of an object or objects by their original owner. The second is deliberate, when the original owner made a conscious decision to bury their own personal possessions, or in some cases those belonging to others. This means that they no longer viewed these objects as having a place in their lives at the particular point in time when the burial took place. In some cases, they might have decided to retrieve them later, and may or may not have been successful. When archaeological finds are rediscovered in modern times, it is our task to work out which explanation best fits the find in question: this can sometimes be reasonably straightforward, and at other times very difficult.

Accidental loss

Everybody at some time in their lives will have lost something, whether a five pence piece dropped in a rush to buy an Underground ticket, or a wedding ring lost whilst helping the children dig sandcastles on the beach. Both of these are examples of accidental loss. Where they differ is in the consequent action taken once the loss has occurred, which will depend upon the attachment felt by the individual to that particular object. In the case of the five pence piece, it is highly unlikely that anyone would feel greatly aggrieved at having lost it. If rushing for the train, they may not even realise that the coin was lost, as it is of such low value, and even if they did, it is by no means certain that they would necessarily stoop to retrieve it.

In contrast, it is extremely unlikely that someone might lose an important item like a wedding ring and not be concerned. They would feel extremely upset by the loss, and would probably take all the steps possible to retrieve the item. There are two reasons for this: the financial value of the item, as wedding rings are usually made from a precious material such as gold; and the sentimental value – a personal emotional attachment to the object. So they would scrabble around in the sand frantically searching for it, ask others to assist in the search, and may even ask a metal detectorist to help them retrieve it. Some metal detecting groups even offer a free service to people who have lost such valuable items, and when these groups have been successful local papers will often pick up the story.

Accidental loss could just as easily have happened in the past, although people did not have the luxury of metal detectors as a last resort for retrieval. The same factors as today would have determined the subsequent action taken by the owner to try to find the object, namely financial and sentimental value: far more time and effort would have been put into retrieving higher value objects such as gold finger-rings than low value objects such as small copper coins. Not surprisingly, therefore, on archaeological sites lower value objects such as a broken copper brooch are far more likely to be found than gold or silver objects.

The chances of discovering precious objects accidentally lost in the past are thus relatively low, but can happen when the retrieval of such objects was difficult for the owner. For example, if a gold coin were accidentally dropped on a recently swept floor, it could easily be seen and picked up. But if the owner were unfortunate enough to drop his or her coin into a cesspit, it would not only be hard to spot, but would also be extremely unpleasant to retrieve. In this instance, the owner may decide that the unpleasantness of the task of retrieval outweighs the benefits of getting the coin back and so decide to abandon it. It therefore enters the archaeological record which gives it the potential to be rediscovered at a later date.

Away from a domestic setting, accidental losses would again depend on circumstance. In a crowded marketplace, coins and other objects could easily be dropped by mistake and quickly become trampled into the ground by others. Thus, even if the finder subsequently realised what had happened, it is highly unlikely that they would be able to go back and find their artefact. Objects could also be lost when moving around the country. Parts of a wagon wheel could easily come off and be lost if the driver hit a particularly deep rut in the track – these were times long before smooth tarmac roads. People could similarly easily lose items if they fell from their horse whilst riding, or simply whilst walking along a country lane. Some people even wore amulets to try to protect themselves from such accidents (see p. 129). Perhaps the most famous accidental loss of all is that of King John's treasure, supposedly lost in the Wash in Norfolk in 1216 (see box opposite).

Deliberate burial

Accidental loss can sometimes lead to the recovery in modern times of some spectacular individual objects, such as the Middleham jewel (now in the Yorkshire Museum) and the Buntingford figurine (see p. 90), both of which were probably lost in this manner. However, most archaeological objects found their way into the archaeological record not by accident, but by the deliberate actions of people in the past.

Deliberate burial was carried out either as a permanent act, when the person burying the object or objects did not wish the finds ever to be retrieved; or, alternatively, as a temporary means of hiding material for subsequent recovery. Archaeologists often have to decide the reasons behind such burial, and in many cases it is far from clear-cut.

Deliberate discard or abandonment

Some objects in the past were simply thrown away or abandoned – this is the origin of the phrase 'archaeology is rubbish'.[1] Most field archaeologists spend their working lives sifting through rubbish left by people in antiquity. Our ancestors did not have refuse collections and landfill sites a long way away from urban areas, so they usually dug a pit, often (but not always) away from where they lived, into which they threw their waste. Alternatively, they used a nearby ditch or well which had fallen out of use. Once full, they would then just cover it up, as much as anything to reduce unpleasant aromas. Anything which had become useless in the eyes of the owner could be thrown into a pit, but refuse tends to be skewed towards certain types of archaeological evidence which we might consider to be of 'lower value'. This includes items such as animal bone, broken bits of pottery and oyster shells. But metalwork might also be discarded, for example a broken brooch which had already been repaired one too many times.

Mythical treasures and ghostly apparitions

'Desire for gold is the prime motive in many a fairytale. . . . Early modern people sought out fairies and begged them to work their magic, not in the interests of morality or soul uplift, but as a way of getting rich. . . . Why do fairies offer special knowledge of treasure? Three reasons: their association with ancient monuments, and hence with the kind of places where people might expect to find it; their link with the dead, and hence with knowledge of the dead, and their association with wild places, places where finders are keepers, and especially with underground caves; this means they know about buried treasure in particular.'[2]

There are many stories about mythical treasures which can be found in folklore traditions throughout the world. Sometimes these stories remain pure fantasy, whilst others seem to have some basis in fact because subsequently the treasures in question come to light. A few of these curious tales are recounted in this chapter.

King John's treasure

Perhaps the most famous story of all is that of King John's treasure, supposedly lost in the Wash in 1216. King John (r. 1199–1216) is best known for signing the *Magna Carta* at Runnymede in June 1215, in which he promised to limit his authority and observe set procedures in government and law. When John went back on this agreement in 1216, the English barons rebelled. During this war, John is supposed to have lost his treasure as he was attempting to cross the Wash in Lincolnshire when his carriage was caught by the rising tide. At some point, probably long after the event, this became a tale of a mythical lost treasure lying buried in the sands of the Wash. The treasure is often thought to be John's Crown Jewels. Even today there are those who believe that, with the right research, it will be possible to establish exactly where the loss occurred and recover the treasure.

It is, however, highly unlikely that John lost any of his treasure, which would have consisted not of the Crown Jewels, but of barrels of silver pennies and a stock of silver plate being carried with his travelling household. The reference to this event comes from the contemporary historian Roger of Wendover's assertion that '*regium apparatum amisit*' ('royal equipment/furnishings/apparel was lost'). This has undoubtedly been misinterpreted by subsequent generations, since the Latin word *apparatus* was not applied to treasure: the lost objects were far more likely to have been relatively minor royal baggage, such as furniture, tents and military equipment. The extensive financial records of the time[3] show no sign of any losses of treasure – quite the reverse, since John had been very successful in the north and East Anglia and was delightedly sending to his various castle treasuries the large sums given in fines by former rebels who had made peace.

Some things which people threw away in the past surprise us. Recently it has been argued that Roman coins were dumped in rubbish pits or ditches when they were no longer usable currency.[4] Yet maybe this should not shock us too much – any hunt through the average rubbish bin in a suburban neighbourhood would, I imagine, reveal all sorts of discarded modern-day items which to some people's eyes are far from being 'rubbish'.

Items that were considered refuse by people in the past can be very useful when rediscovered by us. Pottery is hugely important to archaeologists looking to understand where and how people lived at all periods in history. Whole sets of people who might

Visions and dreams of treasure

Sometimes there are accounts of individuals dreaming about treasure finds or having visions of great wealth being found in a certain place. One of the earliest accounts dates to AD 1288:

> 'In those days near to Wroxeter in a place called Bilebury, the Devil, summoned up by a conjurer, appeared to a certain boy and showed him vases and a ship and a house with an immense quantity of gold.'[5]

In this instance, we do not know of course whether this vision was followed up by any excavation of the supposed place where the treasure was located. A much later account of the nineteenth century however – again near Wroxeter – tells of a dream which seemingly did result in the finding of a treasure hoard:

> 'Betty Fox . . . was the wife of a wheel-wright of Wroxeter. She was an imaginative woman and was convinced like many others before her of the existence of treasure buried in or near the site of the Roman city. She grubbed about in the ruins for treasure by day, which must have been bad for her domestic arrangements; and she dreamed of it by night, which must have been equally fatal to the peaceful slumbers of her presumably hard working spouse. One night she dreamt of a crock of money buried by an alder bush growing upon the bank of the side of the lane which leads from Wroxeter to the Horse Shoe Inn at Uckington . . . she awoke, went out, started digging, hit an urn, and found over 400 Roman silver coins [probably denarii, the standard Roman coinage of the first and second centuries AD]; [which she] sold to different collectors; she received £28, a good sum in those days.'[6]

Interestingly, the account suggests that there had been a local folklore tradition that a hoard had been buried nearby, which seems to be a recurring theme with many discoveries of treasure.

The pedlar of Swaffham

The story of the pedlar of Swaffham is one of the most famous tales of treasure known from English folklore. The following account dates to 1699:

> 'Constant tradition says that there lived in former times in Soffham [Swaffham], *alias* Sopham, in Norfolk, a certain pedlar, who dreamed that if he went to London Bridge, and stood there,

he should hear very joyfull newse, which he at first sleighted, but afterwards, his dream being doubled and trebled upon him, he resolved to try the issue of it, and accordingly went to London, and stood on the bridge there two or three days, looking about him, but heard nothing that might yield him any comfort. At last it happened that a shopkeeper there, hard by, having noted his fruitless standing, seeing that he neither sold any wares nor asked any almes, went to him and most earnestly begged to know what he wanted there, or what his business was; to which the pedlar honestly answered that he had dreamed that if he came to London and stood there upon the bridge he should hear good newse; at which the shopkeeper laughed heartily, asking him if he was such a fool as to take a journey on such a silly errand, adding: "I'll tell thee, country fellow, last night I dreamed that I was at Sopham, in Norfolk, a place utterly unknown to me, where methought behind a pedlar's house in a certain orchard, and under a great oak tree, if I digged I should find a vast treasure. Now think you," says he, "that I am such a fool to take such a long journey upon me upon the instigation of a silly dream? No, no, I'm wiser. Therefore, good fellow, learn wit from me, and get you home, and mind your business." The pedlar observing his words, what he had say'd he dream'd, and knowing they concentred in him, glad of such joyfull newse, went speedily home, and digged and found a prodigious great treasure, with which he grew exceeding rich; and Soffham [Church] being for the most part fallen down, he set on workmen and rectified it most sumptuously, at his own charges; and to this day there is his statue therein, but in stone, with his pack at his back and his dogg at his heels; and his memory is also preserved by the same form or picture in most of the old glass windows, taverns, and alehouses of that town unto this day.'[7]

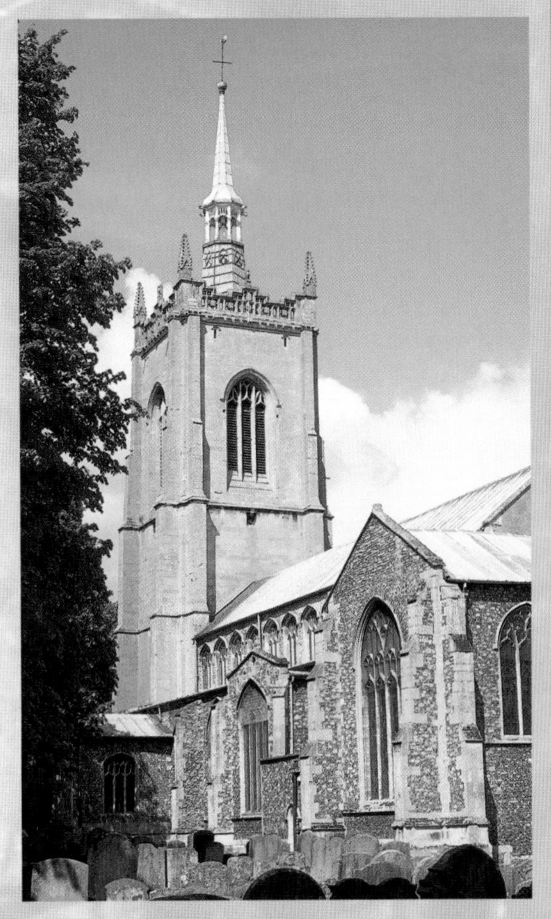

16 The church at Swaffham, for which the pedlar John Chapman financed the building of the north aisle (above); and a pew inside the church (opposite), carved in his image.

As noted in the account, the pedlar seems to have used his new-found wealth to help with the rebuilding of his local church. And the story does seem to have some basis in fact: the pedlar in the story was one John Chapman (the surname Chapman means pedlar), who was church warden at Swaffham in 1462, and who is known to have financed the building of the north aisle (fig. 16) . Indeed, some of the stained glass windows in the church today are thought to show John Chapman and his wife.

previously have been frustratingly elusive to archaeologists, such as Viking settlers (see p. 110), can suddenly make their presence known by the simple discovery of a discarded brooch with a broken pin. Rubbish, therefore, should not be underestimated.

Deliberate burial in a grave

When archaeological objects, which can range from gold earrings to a simple pottery beaker, are found with the remains of a burial, it is clear that the persons carrying out the burial never intended the finds to be recovered at a future date. Good examples of this are the objects in the grave of the recently discovered Amesbury archer which included over a hundred personal possessions of the deceased man (see p. 53). Many past societies carried out such mortuary practices and buried prized personal possessions with their owners in the belief that the spirit of these inanimate objects passed into the next world too. Another very famous example of this is the Sutton Hoo ship burial, the highly elaborate burial of an Anglo-Saxon king (see p. 15).

In both these examples, discovery in modern times can tell us a huge amount about life at the time and the rituals of death and burial. But the people carrying out the burial had no intention of providing us with this information – they were simply honouring their deceased in the best way they knew. Despite this, it is better that these items are not left untouched if discovered, as long as it is ensured that the objects and the remains of the deceased are treated with respect. This is because it is possible that such finds might be recovered illicitly (see Chapter 5), as has often happened in the past. In other cases, excavation of burials is often necessary when the site in question is to be destroyed by new construction work.

Deliberate ritual deposition

The burial of objects with the remains of the dead is a characteristic of ritual deposition but by no means the only one. Objects were also buried in the ground for other ritual purposes, either as individual artefacts or as one of a group. This is an area of archaeological study that continues to be debated as it is always difficult to comprehend the motives of people in the past. In order to understand such finds, it is vital that archaeologists look very closely at their contents, compare them with other similar finds and, wherever possible, conduct research on the sites at which they were discovered.

Good examples of possible ritual deposition of treasure objects include the Snettisham torc burials (see p. 137) and the Winchester gold jewellery (see p. 59). In both instances, the circumstances under which the finds were buried, and the places which were chosen for burial, seems to suggest that they were made as ritual offerings. These might have been made to appease the gods, in circumstances such as a tragedy within the community, like the death of a child. Alternatively, they might have been made in order to try to manipulate future events, such as ensuring a good harvest, or a less severe winter. In these cases, a community's most treasured possessions might have been perceived as the means of achieving the desired outcome.

We seldom know the exact rituals which surrounded such burials, but in some cases they may have been very elaborate. The 'sacrifice' of precious objects, particularly in prehistoric times, may have been accompanied by the sacrifice of animals and occasionally even humans, and would have been enacted in places regarded as special or sacred. In Iron Age Britain, for instance, these may have been certain types of high wooded places in the landscape – archaeologists believe that the fabled 'sacred grove' really did exist.

Sometimes archaeological or natural features are found in association with treasure objects which make it clear that a sacred place has been deliberately chosen for deposition. Temple structures, such as the square Roman temple found at Wanborough (see p. 142), often produce precious objects deposited deliberately as offerings to a range of deities. Special natural places in the landscape were also favoured places to make offerings. Examples include natural springs, such as the famous hot springs at Bath in Somerset, which would often have either simple or elaborate temple structures built around them. The idea of casting objects into sacred waters dates back to prehistory, and even persists to this day – the 'wishing well' or fountain, such as the Trevi fountain in Rome, is a modern-day continuation.

Without an obvious ritual context such as a temple, deposits made on land are often difficult to interpret as definitely 'ritual' in nature. The Snettisham torcs, for example, although interpreted by some as being ritual deposits, might simply have been buried

Mythical treasures and ghostly apparitions

The Rillaton Cup

The Rillaton cup (fig. 17) dates to the early Bronze Age (*c.* 1900–1600 BC) and is very similar to the cup found recently at Ringlemere (see p. 55). Like the Mold cape (see box p. 42) it too has a ghost story associated with it.[8] The cup was found in about 1837 in a grave during excavations at Rillaton manor on Bodmin Moor in Cornwall. For hundreds of years the local moor was said to be haunted by the ghost of a Druid priest. The ghost would emerge from a nearby barrow and offer passers-by a golden cup which contained a magic potion. When the traveller drank from the cup it was impossible to drain the cup dry. During one of these supposed encounters the traveller was said to have thrown the remaining liquid in the spectre's face, and soon afterwards he had an accident on his horse and both died. It is not clear if sightings of the Druid stopped after the Rillaton cup had been excavated.

17 The Rillaton gold cup, Cornwall, early Bronze Age. The cup is one of a number of treasure discoveries which has a ghost story linked with it.

in a location which allowed them to be an easily accessible source of bullion. There are instances, though, when precious objects were put beyond the reach of recovery, which in Britain usually means deposition in deep water. In these circumstances we can be fairly sure that there were ritual motives behind the act. Good examples of this are the large number of shields and weapons which were cast into the Thames, such as the Battersea shield (fig. 18). Even here, however, interpretation can be difficult. Some believe that arms and armour were often thrown away after battle, perhaps to ensure that they were not seized by the enemy. Accidental loss in water is also a possibility, as crossing rivers or waterlogged ground, for example during flooding, could be extremely hazardous. This is where the myth of King John's treasure arose (see box p. 35). Water was also sometimes used as a hiding place for valuables – some finds dating to post-medieval Scandinavia consist of leather bags hidden in water and attached to a nearby tree to allow recovery.[9]

18 The Battersea shield, *c.* 350–50 BC, found in the Thames. Like other weapons and armour of the Iron and Bronze Ages, it was probably cast into the river as a form of ritual sacrifice.

Deposition for safekeeping or savings

People often buried their precious objects for safekeeping or as savings. In ancient times the security of personal belongings could not be ensured (or insured, for that matter). The theft of valuables in the past is well attested. For example, in the Roman period, some temple sites have produced lead curses, which often have an inscription entreating the gods to bring bad fortune on the thief of some treasured personal item.

Individuals might bury objects, or groups of objects, in a place known only to them because they were often not secure in the home or even in public buildings. The best example of this can be found in the diary of Samuel Pepys (1633–1703). Pepys was reacting to the burning of the ship the Royal Charles by the Dutch at Chatham Docks during the so-called Second Dutch War. Like many other Londoners, he was very fearful that the dispute would escalate, and thus sought a way of hiding his wealth. He is quite open about his fears in his diary entry for 12–13 June 1667:

> 'And the truth is, I do fear so much that the whole kingdom is undone, that I do this night resolve to study with my father and wife what to do with the little that I have in money by me. . . . [The next day, after discussions with his wife and father] I presently resolved of my father's and wife's going into the country; and at two hours warning they did go by the coach this day – with about 1300*l* [pounds] in gold in their nightbag; pray God give them good passage and good care to hide it when they come home, but my heart is full of fear.'[10]

Later on Pepys refers again to the burial of his coins, this time providing details of the actual circumstances surrounding this. This entry comes from 19–20 June 1667:

> 'They being gone [two visitors to Pepys's home], I and my wife to talk; who did give me so bad an account of her and my father's method in burying our gold, that made me mad – and she herself is not pleased with it, she believing that my sister knows of it. My father and she did it on Sunday when they were gone to church [the rest of the family] in open daylight in the midst of the garden, where for aught they knew, many eyes might see them; which put me in such trouble, that I was almost mad about it, and presently cast about how to have it back again to secure it here, the times being a little better now; at least at Whitehall they seem

Mythical treasures and ghostly apparitions

THE MOLD GOLD CAPE

The Mold cape (fig. 19) was discovered in 1833 by workmen quarrying for stone, and is now on permanent display at the British Museum. It is an unparalleled object, beaten from a single ingot of gold, and dates to the early Bronze Age (*c.* 1900–1600 BC).

The field in which the Mold cape was found is known in Welsh as Bryn-yr-Ellyllon, which translates as 'Goblin's or Fairies' Hill'. Fairies have often been associated with the protection of treasure (see quotation in box p. 35), but it is probably most likely that the name came simply from the fact that the field contained an ancient burial mound. However, the discovery of the cape had nonetheless been preceded eight years earlier by a local account of a ghostly figure seen apparently wearing it:

> 'One night, apparently about the year 1825, an elderly and respectable Welsh-woman walked into Mold to retrieve – good wife that she was – her husband from a public house in the town, and lead him home. They started back late at night. The way they took was from the old Mold and Chester road, which about a quarter of a mile from the town at that time skirted the southern slope of a barrow – the Bryn-yr-Ellyllon, or Goblin's Hill – one of several such that lay at a little distance from the river Alun, which flows through the vale of Mold. Just as they reached this spot the woman perceived a figure "of unusual size, and clothed in a coat of gold, which shone like the sun". This figure crossed the road before her and then vanished as it reached the Goblin's Hill. . . . The matter was very generally bruited about the district.'[11]

In 1833, the vision appeared to be vindicated, as the Mold cape was discovered when parts of the Goblin's Hill were used to fill a hole caused by nearby road repairs. Even more interestingly, when the cape was initially acquired by the British Museum in 1836, it was interpreted as an elaborate horse harness-fitting, or peytrel, worn across a horse's chest. But as more pieces of the cape were gradually acquired by the Museum (it had initially been split up between the different workmen who discovered it), it became clear that this elucidation was incorrect. The British Museum's conservation department was able to reconstruct the cape to show that it was in fact an ovular object beaten from a single piece of gold which would have been worn over the shoulders of a man or woman, probably on ceremonial occasions (fig. 20). This means that in fact it was far more similar in function to the 'coat of gold' seen in the apparition experienced by the woman back in 1825.

19 ***Above*** **The Mold gold cape, Flintshire, north Wales, early Bronze Age. This unique ceremonial cape was apparently seen being worn by a ghost a number of years prior to its discovery.**

20 An artist's impression of how the Mold cape might have looked when worn.

as if they were – but one way or other, I am resolved to free them from the place if I can get them. Such was my trouble at this, that I fell out with my wife; that though new come to town, I did not sup with her nor speak to her tonight, but to bed and sleep.'[12]

Pepys had a rather traumatic experience recovering his hoard. It not only took him a long time to locate where it had been buried, but he also had to do this under cover of darkness. He did eventually recover all but about thirty pieces of his treasure.[13]

Such burial of coins and precious objects was however practised long before the seventeenth century. The problem is that in these cases, we may have the objects, but we do not have a neat written account, like that of Pepys, of the exact reason for burial. Thus it is usually not clear what the exact motives were, and different interpretations may be put forward.

Times of crisis are one instance, however, when we can be fairly certain of the reasons for burial. In such periods in history, people buried their precious possessions because they did not want others to find them. They may have done this in haste, for instance if they knew that the nearby village had just been attacked by an invading force and that they were probably next; or in a planned manner, because they had to leave their home for a certain period and did not feel that it would be secure in their absence. Thus, during the English Civil Wars, a number of coin hoards seem to have been buried before new recruits left for battle or as a reaction to those troubled times (see p. 92). Because the original owners never returned to recover them – we can only assume they met a sticky end – when they are rediscovered in more recent times, these hoards can be closely tied in with this particular historical event.

But being able to tie together a time of crisis such as the English Civil Wars and finds of treasure is quite rare. For many treasure finds, particularly of the Roman and prehistoric periods, this is far more difficult. Although times of crisis are known, it does not necessarily follow that finds of treasure will be connected with them. One example of this is the Boudiccan revolt in AD 60 when the ancient Britons, under the leadership of the Icenian queen Boudicca, sacked a number of Roman towns in protest against Roman rule. In East Anglia, the main source of the rebellion, a number of coin hoards have been discovered which date broadly to this period. Therefore it might seem logical to assume that they were buried by people involved in the revolt, who never returned to recover them – in a very similar manner to the Civil War hoards of the seventeenth century. This may well explain why these hoards were buried, but it is by no means certain that this is the only explanation. The problem is that firstly, the coin hoards cannot be proven all to be of the same date, and could have been buried over a period of twenty or so years. Secondly, the area as a whole produces a large number of treasure finds of prehistoric and Roman date, which may mean that there was a local tradition of burying finds in this manner – nothing to do with times of crisis, more just part of everyday life.

Thus, in order to make a strong case for burial for safekeeping, individual finds need to be examined in great detail if clues are to be found which might suggest this. Unfortunately, in many cases of discoveries of treasure, the background to the burial – the archaeological context – is not sufficiently well documented to make such a judgement.

An exception is the Hoxne treasure (see p. 78), which we know was very carefully buried in a large chest with the objects neatly packed and protected. This must imply that the owners had every intention of returning to recover it, although why they did not we shall never know.

How finds are discovered

We have seen how finds could have ended up in the ground, either by accident, design, or deliberate discard. From any point onwards, it was perfectly possible for these objects to be discovered and dug up. This could have been the result of knowledge of their whereabouts, the person or people who originally buried the material being the most likely to enact retrieval. Knowledge of possessions such as treasure could also have been passed to others, for example when someone was on their deathbed or imprisoned. In these cases, the owner is seeking to ensure that their precious possessions pass to relatives or loved ones rather than be lost forever or found by chance by strangers.

Chance discovery

If not recovered by the original owners or relatives, subsequent chance discovery was probably the commonest way in which many archaeological finds, particularly treasure, were discovered in the past. This could have been the result of agricultural work, such as ploughing: the Mildenhall treasure was unearthed exactly in this manner (see p. 71). Extraction of minerals or natural raw materials such as peat can also result in the discovery of treasure. Often this happens well away from settlements, which in turn has made them attractive places for people to bury objects in the first place. Sometimes, however, finds have been made much closer to home, with small coin hoards found in the walls of old houses when renovation work is being conducted (see box opposite).

The treatment of treasure objects when discovered in the past is probably often rather unpalatable to modern archaeologists, and some examples of this have already been recounted (see p. 12). In the twenty-first century, most people recognise that it is important for all archaeological finds to be treated with care and respect, and preserved and studied so that everyone can enjoy them. In the past this was often not the case. Precious metal objects were frequently melted down, with their bullion value being viewed as their primary attribute, and their historical and archaeological value not even considered. We should perhaps not be too judgemental, though, as these were often difficult times; and in the case of finders of precious metal, the bullion value of the objects could have meant that their lives were changed for ever.

An example of the regrettable treatment of a treasure find was reported in the journal *Archaeologia* in 1832. The find was undoubtedly spectacular, consisting of twelve Iron Age gold torcs found in Brittany, France. The torcs were sold to a local watchmaker who then offered them to various museums. As the anonymous author in *Archaeologia* recounts:

Treasure in the attic

Very occasionally, finds of treasure are made in people's own homes right under their noses, usually when old houses are being renovated. Sometimes wall cavities were used as places to conceal precious objects, usually coins, and these may have been forgotten or not retrieved because the owner died before being able to do so.

One such instance concerns a gold coin hoard found during the reign of Henry VIII in about AD 1543. An account dating from this time runs as follows:

> 'And [the jurors present] that on the fifth day of January in the 33rd year of the reign of the said present lord king of Lamarsh . . . a certain free tenement of Robert Laye came to be accidentally burnt down. And that by the same reason some treasure was found concealed of old and in a secret hole within a certain clay partition wall of the aforesaid tenement, the sum of £27 5s sterling in gold, all of the coinage of Henry VI, lately king of England, of any owner of which the aforesaid jurors are ignorant.'[14]

This sum was a considerable amount for this time – £20 would have been enough to build a sizeable house – and probably represented the life savings of a wealthy local farmer or merchant.

A more recent example is a hoard of silver coins dating to the reign of Charles II (1660–85), found by an electrician in the loft of a house in Burton Overy, Leicestershire, in 1994.[15]

The window-box hoard

One of the most unusual findspots for a hoard of treasure, in this instance late Roman silver coins, was recorded in the early 1950s.[16] They were said to have been found in the earth within a window-box in a flat in St Pancras, north London. If the story is genuine, the soil containing the coins must have been dug up in a clump, from a location which will always remain a mystery, and deposited in the window-box, with their precious contents at the time unknown.

> 'There were hopes that a treasure so important to antiquarian knowledge might have been preserved. I have since learned with regret that, no purchaser appearing, the whole of this splendid collection has been consigned to the crucible!'

Other finders of treasure were often very reluctant to give up their discoveries. Mr Ford kept the Mildenhall treasure for four years before finally being persuaded to declare it (see p. 72). His feelings on the matter are made clear in a letter in which he states, with some indignation: 'I reported the find to the police at Mildenhall in the 21st inst., who promptly came and pinched the lot.'[17]

Deliberate hunting

Antiquarian tomb raiders

Aside from chance, deliberate hunting for treasure has been practised for centuries. In addition to the occasional discovery resulting from a dream or vision (see box pp. 36–7), more practical methods were usually employed to hunt for archaeological finds. Clues in the landscape were used as indications of possible locations of treasure. These would usually be in the form of mounds of earth or barrows, which were sometimes used during the prehistoric and early medieval periods as the burial chambers of important members of society (fig. 21). Digging into such places would have potentially been disappointing, as they often did not contain anything other than the bones of the deceased and perhaps some pottery, but in some cases more valuable items might have been found. A recent example is the Ringlemere gold cup (see p. 55), which, thankfully, was properly reported when found by a metal detectorist, but could just as easily have been discovered and stolen by someone else previously. Still today in some countries, many individuals make money by ransacking known areas where there are high concentrations of ancient tombs. In parts of Italy and Sicily, the *tombaroli* are a well-established group of 'professional' tomb raiders who make their living out of retrieving objects from burials and selling them on the illicit antiquities market.[18]

21 Silbury Hill, Wiltshire. Although it is the largest prehistoric barrow known in Britain, no burials have ever been found in it. Clues like mounds in the landscape were often used by people over the centuries when attempting to locate where treasure might be buried.

Metal detecting and fieldwalking

Deliberate targeting of ancient barrows unfortunately probably still goes on in Britain, but these sites are protected by law, and such activity is generally rare. Most amateur hunting these days means random metal detecting, and the popularity of the hobby

22 'Seahenge', a prehistoric timber circle reported by an amateur beachcomber at Holme, Norfolk. It is an excellent example of the public's role in making important archaeological discoveries, and demonstrates that these can be sites as well as artefacts.

has already been highlighted (see p. 18). Metal detecting is essentially a modern extension of fieldwalking and beachcombing, activities which have a long history in Britain. Fieldwalking is a standard technique used by professional archaeologists when conducting surveys (see box p. 48), but alongside beachcombing has been practised by amateurs for hundreds of years. In the nineteenth century, for example, Mary Anning became one of the most well-known amateur beachcombers. Her fossil discoveries on the beaches of Dorset were key to the discovery of the dinosaurs, even if others carried out the research on them.[19] Although Anning gained financially – in reality very modestly – from her supply of fossils to keen palaeontologists, she was initially motivated by a simple desire to discover objects from a distant age. Beachcombers and artefact hunters on river foreshores (the Thames Mudlarks, for instance; see p. 119) have for centuries discovered not just fossils but important flint objects (see p. 99) and even abandoned ancient structures such as Seahenge (fig. 22).[20] Metal detecting is an extension of these activities which takes advantage of modern technology, as it allows the position of buried finds to be located in addition to those spotted with the naked eye.

Most amateur artefact hunters will say that the main attraction of finding objects made by ancient hands is the feeling of connection it gives them with people in the past. They often remark that the thrill comes from being the first to have touched the object since its burial. Many will also have a good knowledge of local history which they use as a guide to their searches. Few, however, would deny that there is a financial motivation involved, although those who persevere accept that the likelihood of discovering a valuable treasure find is of similarly low odds to winning the lottery.

The Portable Antiquities Scheme (see p. 27) was set up to promote good links with metal detectorists and other amateurs to provide an opportunity to record their finds. But another facet of the project which should not be overlooked is the protection which the Scheme affords to our heritage. In England and Wales, some archaeological sites are protected by law as Scheduled Ancient Monuments, and digging into them is strictly forbidden. In addition, under planning guidelines, anyone carrying out construction work which will destroy significant archaeological deposits is obliged to pay for archaeological excavation. But this protection does not extend to agricultural land, and every year more and more archaeological sites are damaged and even destroyed by ploughing and other methods of cultivation.[21] Agricultural machines often dig deep into undisturbed archaeological layers, churning them up and bringing any archaeological material contained within them into the surface ploughsoil. This means that the archaeological context of these objects is lost forever. In addition, the effects of changing temperature and moisture levels in ploughsoil can also cause metal objects in particular to deteriorate, and there is also anecdotal evidence that farm chemicals, such as pesticides, have a negative effect on metalwork. Therefore finds made by metal detectorists might be the only evidence left of underlying archaeology and the Portable Antiquities Scheme offers some way in which these important clues to our past can be recorded before they disappear forever.

Fieldwalking

Fieldwalking is an archaeological technique which involves people carefully walking across ploughed fields on a planned grid, and picking up and recording any ancient artefacts they find. These might be flint tools or debitage from making flints, sherds of broken pottery, pieces of brick and tile, or even parts of a Roman mosaic. It differs from metal detecting because no additional help, beyond a keen eye, is used to aid the search. What is discovered, and in particular where the discoveries are made, is carefully recorded. These results are then plotted on a map. These maps can help show where people lived at different times in the past and, on a smaller scale, what might have been happening in different parts of a Roman villa or medieval village. This can be compared with other evidence such as aerial photographs, the results of geophysical surveys and systematic metal detecting to create a more detailed picture. An important site in Leicestershire, dating to the late Iron Age, was discovered in precisely this manner (see p. 65). All the members of the group who discovered this site were amateurs, giving up their spare time to learn more about the history of their local area through fieldwalking.

Rescue archaeology

It is certainly the case that the majority of treasure finds, and indeed many important non-treasure discoveries, are made by amateur metal detectorists and fieldwalkers. Indeed, in a recent publication of treasure finds,[22] over 95 per cent were made in precisely this manner. But the fact that professional archaeologists also uncover important treasure finds must not be overlooked. Most archaeological work in Britain today is rescue work ahead of development, for example the building of a new housing estate; and sometimes treasure – as legally defined – is found as a result. An example is the Amesbury archer (see p. 53), found during the building of a new school on Boscombe Down, Wiltshire.

At the beginning of this chapter, the importance of context was heavily emphasised (see p. 32). Without a good context for an archaeological find, whether treasure or otherwise, the amount we can learn about it is substantially reduced. Professional archaeologists are trained to understand archaeological contexts. Therefore, although

23 Excavation of a hoard of Iron Age metalwork in Hertfordshire. The reporting of the site by a metal detectorist allowed it to be excavated by professionals.

most treasure finds are made by amateurs, the ones which we know most about are those that have subsequently been investigated by archaeologists. Sometimes it has taken a huge amount of detective work to discover the location of the find, as was the case with the Salisbury hoard (see p. 144); in other instances the finder has had the good sense to call in professionals at an early stage, such as when the Hoxne treasure was discovered (see p. 78). In an ideal world, professionals should investigate all finds of treasure (fig. 23). Dialogue between amateur finders and professionals is vital for this to occur: our past is fragile and precious and we must all work together to protect and understand it (see p. 150 for practical guidelines).

Conclusion

This chapter has demonstrated the many ways in which archaeological finds, including treasure, became buried, and the equally large number of ways in which they were subsequently rediscovered. These discoveries are nothing, however, unless we seek to understand what they are telling us about the past. That is the subject of the next chapter.

3

Treasure Tells Stories

Introduction

Britain has produced many major treasure finds over the centuries, with the pace of discovery quickening particularly since the advent of the metal detector (see Chapters 1 and 2). The earliest treasure finds as defined by laws in England and Wales come from the late Neolithic, such as those found in association with the Amesbury archer (see pp. 53–5); thereafter they come from all historical periods, some better represented than others. But treasure in the wider sense does not just mean finds of gold and silver: equally important are discoveries of stone tools, such as one of the earliest known hand-axes found on a Norfolk beach (see p. 99), which are hugely influential to our understanding of the early history of our ancestors.

The discovery of treasure continues to attract a huge amount of media attention, and thus often constitutes a fascinating story in its own right. Tales of discovery can range from those which are well documented, straightforward and widely accepted, such as the recent Winchester gold (see p. 59), to those which continue to cause disagreement and even incredulity to this day, such as the Mildenhall treasure (see p. 71). But it is the stories which these treasures can tell about our past that really matter as they allow us a rare insight into cultures, attitudes and beliefs. Some of the stories of major treasure discoveries are recounted here. The treasures in this chapter have been arranged in broadly historical order, and run from the Bronze and Iron Ages of British prehistory, through the Roman and early medieval periods, and finish with the troubled times of the English Civil Wars of the seventeenth century AD.

Treasures from Bronze and Iron Age Britain

The Bronze Age (*c.* 2200–700 BC) and Iron Age (*c.* 700 BC–AD 43) were times of huge change within the British Isles. The main development was the discovery and exploitation of metal ores, initially of copper and tin to form bronze, and later iron which, though more difficult to work, began to be used alongside bronze to make more robust objects. The technology to work these raw materials provided our early ancestors with greater versatility in shaping their environment, and seems to have given many individuals greater power and status within their communities. Techniques were also developed throughout the course of these periods to work precious metals such as gold and silver, with early simple sheet objects superseded by the end of the period by highly skilled and refined metalworking methods.

The Bronze and Iron Ages are known as prehistoric times because no written documents survive, apart from the writings at the end of the period by outsiders such as the Roman general Julius Caesar. Yet, despite the lack of written evidence, there is nonetheless a wealth of archaeological remains which can tell us stories about these periods, some of the most spectacular of which are recounted here. All the discoveries in this section were made in the last four years, and demonstrate the dynamic nature of archaeology in which new finds are constantly shaping and modifying our understanding of prehistory.

The Amesbury archer: an eye-witness to Stonehenge?

Date of discovery: 2001; date of burial: c. *2400–2200* BC

Many of the treasure finds discussed in this book were discovered accidentally by amateurs, but spectacular discoveries are also made during the course of professional archaeological excavation. One such discovery occurred during the building of a school at Boscombe Down near Amesbury, Wiltshire.[1]

The grave of the 'Amesbury archer', as he has become known, is the most well-furnished burial of the 'Copper' Age (*c.* 2500–2000 BC) yet discovered in Britain (figs 24–5). It contained only two items of precious metal in the form of gold earrings or hair tresses, but under the new Treasure Act (see Chapter 1), all the other items in the grave qualified as treasure as associated objects (see box p. 20).

24 The grave of the Amesbury archer, Wiltshire, prior to full excavation.

The burial, excavated by Wessex Archaeology under the directorship of Andrew Fitzpatrick, was of a man aged between thirty-five and forty-five years. His body had been placed lying on the left side with his legs flexed and his face to the north. Around and on his body was placed a rich array of objects. These included two gold hair tresses, which were placed by his knees; also placed there were a shale 'wristguard', a small tanged copper knife and a ring made of shale, probably from a belt. On his forearm was another 'wristguard' or 'bracer' which is thought to have been used to protect his arm from the recoil of a bowstring. The archer's bow – which led to his nickname – is inferred from a group of fifteen flint arrowheads, and as these were at a higher level than the other finds, they seem to have been scattered over his hips and legs (although it is also possible they had been placed on top of the wooden chamber in which he was buried). In front of the man's face were two beakers, a spatula made of red deer bone for working flint, boars' tusks, a cache of flints, and two more copper knives. More beakers and flints lay behind the man's back and below his posterior and feet. Also behind his back was a 'cushion stone', which could have been used as a small anvil to work metal objects.

The dating of the archer to between 2400 and 2200 BC was based on an examination of the artefacts found with him, and is confirmed by subsequent radiocarbon dating of his bones. This is a very important time in this particular area of the British Isles, as it is the period during which the largest stones at Stonehenge were being erected. This tells us that the archer could have been an eyewitness to the raising of the stones, or

25 An artist's impression of how the Amesbury archer might have looked.

was possibly even involved in the process, although we will certainly never be sure of the part he might have played. Nevertheless, it must be significant that the burial was made near to well-known monuments of this region, not just Stonehenge, but also Woodhenge and the Durrington Walls. The find is also interesting because it is somewhat earlier than the main series of burial mounds or barrows for which this area is famous. The archer's burial, in contrast to these later ones, was rather less conspicuous (at least from the outside). A large rectangular grave was dug, and a small timber mortuary chamber might have been placed over the top. No evidence of the timber chamber has survived, but the discovery of a similar chamber from another grave found nearby, excavated in 1960, provides a good parallel.[2] This burial implies that the archer's chamber probably had a set of four timber posts, one at each corner, to support a roof, although it is not clear if this would have been flat or gabled. Planks of wood were placed at the bottom and sides of the burial pit in order to keep the sides from collapsing. Mourners would have placed his body inside this chamber and then added the artefacts, such as the beakers and arrows, around and on top of his body. If an earthen mound also covered the grave, it would have been low in height.

In addition to the archer, another burial was found nearby of a man aged between twenty-five and thirty years, which the excavators thought probably dated to the same period. This was confirmed dramatically when the skeleton was being examined in the laboratory as two more gold hair tresses, exactly like those in the archer's burial, emerged from inside the man's jaw.

Who were these two men and how were they connected? Radiocarbon dating on the second man confirmed that he too had been buried between 2400 and 2200 BC which, when added to the sets of tress rings, encouraged the view that they may have been related. Close examination of the two skeletons also showed that they had many similar physical characteristics, strongly suggesting that this assumption was correct. It seems likely, therefore, that they were father and son. In addition, both were shown to have remarkable connections beyond Wessex. The archer's knives, for example, are made of copper which originated in western France or even Spain. Even more remarkably, analysis of the archer's teeth suggests that he originated in middle Europe, perhaps in the Alps. The analysis of the other grave suggests an origin for him in southern England. Therefore, if he was the archer's son, the archer must have travelled to Britain first before fathering him.

Much more work will need to be conducted on these two hugely important discoveries. The Amesbury archer's nickname derives from the large number of flint arrowheads found with him, but it may be that archery was not his primary skill. The 'cushion stone' found behind his back and used for metalworking, raises the possibility that he himself was a metalworker, and this may account for his high status. The discovery of metal was a huge technological breakthrough, and those possessing the skills to forge weapons and tools from solid rock would have undoubtedly been held in very high esteem. Perhaps this is why the archer and his son were buried with such ceremony and such riches. Further archaeological work will help to solve the mystery – as is the case with an important gold cup, also of Bronze Age date, recently found in Kent.

The Ringlemere gold cup

Date of discovery: 2001; date of burial: c. *1700–1500* BC

As we have seen, the grave of the Amesbury archer dates to a time when metalworking was first being adopted in Britain. Roughly 700 years later, Britain was at an advanced stage of the early Bronze Age, when the alloying of copper and tin to make bronze for weapons and tools was well established. It is in this world that the Ringlemere cup may be set (fig. 26).

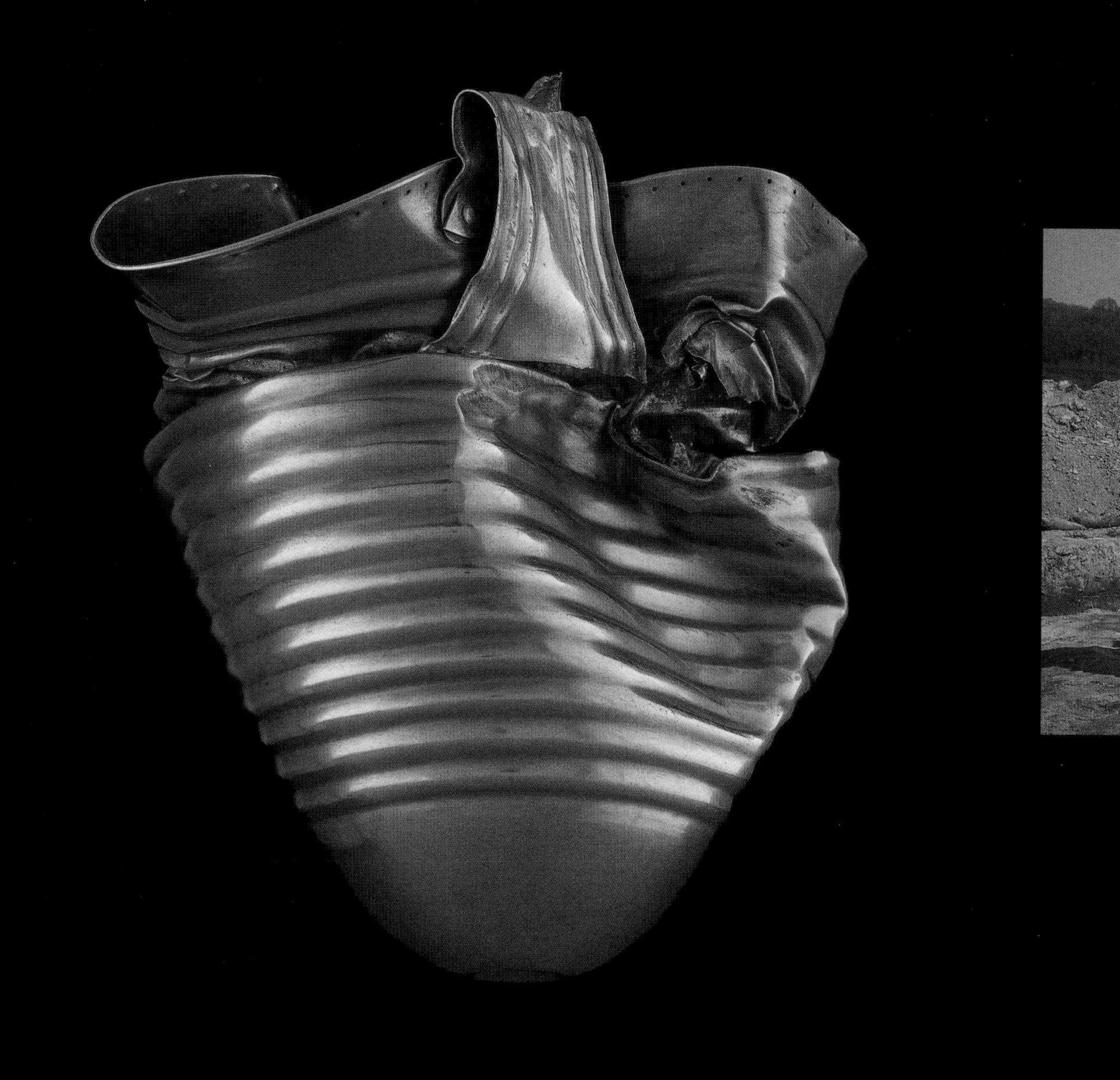

26 The Ringlemere gold cup, found in Kent in 2001.

The background to its discovery is similar to that of many of the recent treasure finds discussed in this book. The cup was found in November 2001 by a metal detectorist, Cliff Bradshaw, in a field near the village of Ringlemere in east Kent (fig. 27). Cliff received an unusually strong signal from his metal detector, and on digging down discovered a gold cup, somewhat crushed. This was very probably because it had been struck by a subsoiling machine, used in modern farming to break up ground to a considerable depth.

Cliff had been studying archaeology as an adult learner. He knew that his find was gold, and probably ancient, and after searching a book at home his suspicions were confirmed when he came across a picture of the only other example known from Britain: the remarkably similar Rillaton cup, found in Cornwall by workmen in 1837 (see box p. 39). Cliff behaved responsibly, reporting his find to Michael Lewis, the Finds Liaison Officer at the time with the Portable Antiquities Scheme in Kent.

Crushed or not, the cup was a remarkable discovery. Gold was a valuable commodity, then as now (see box below). The craftsmanship is superb – the cup was fashioned

Desire for gold

Gold was a highly desirable commodity in the ancient world, as it is indeed today. There are several reasons for this:

- *Rarity* – gold is one of the only metals which occurs in nature in its pure form, but only in small quantities.
- *Working properties* – gold is soft and malleable, making it easy to work and versatile for craftsmen.
- *Eternal properties* – gold is naturally shiny, is the same colour as the sun and never corrodes in its pure form. All these qualities mean that it is associated with an eternal, everlasting quality which no other metal has. This means that throughout the ages it has been identified by many cultures with eternity.

27 Cliff Bradshaw, the finder of the Ringlemere cup (second from right) with Keith Parfitt (Canterbury Archaeological Trust, far left) and the landowners Andrew and Bob Smith.

from a single piece of thick gold sheet, probably using a hammer and former (a shaped block of wood is most likely). The handle, a wide gold strip, was made separately and riveted to the body with the aid of distinctive diamond-shaped washers. In common with the Rillaton example, the body is corrugated and the handle outlined with grooves. It was clear from the beginning that the Ringlemere cup had a sub-conical base, and recent documentary evidence confirmed that the Rillaton cup also had a rounded base at the time of discovery. Thus neither cup could have stood up by itself.

Interesting though the cup is in its own right, it was essential to discover more about the circumstances of its burial (the importance of archaeological context has already been highlighted in Chapter 2). Excavations were set up under the direction of the Canterbury Archaeological Trust with support from English Heritage and the British Museum (fig. 28). These excavations have shown that a very low – indeed barely visible – hump in the ground noticed by Cliff was the ploughed-out remains of a barrow (burial mound), which was surrounded by a substantial circular ditch. The cup was found within the last vestige of the mound, but in a context badly disturbed by animal burrows. As yet, no grave pit or human remains have been found, but fieldwork continues. What we do know, from the aerial photographs, is that we are dealing with a probable Bronze Age cemetery now evidenced only by its circular enclosing ditches. Very few such sites were known in east Kent until relatively recently because of erosion by ploughing for many centuries. Scraped up with the soil making the mound were sherds of pottery (grooved ware) – evidence of still earlier activity during the Later Neolithic period, several centuries before the barrow was constructed.

28 Excavation of the site of the Ringlemere cup. The random lines running across the site are the remains of rabbit burrows. Wherever possible, the sites of major treasure finds are investigated to provide vital information about context.

Early Bronze Age society was engaged in new ways of burying its dead in many parts of Europe. In Britain, a series of richly furnished graves in Wessex (most of the south-central counties of England – Berkshire, Wiltshire, Dorset and Hampshire) and elsewhere tells us that the elite – important individuals in society – were being commemorated. Sometimes these burial mounds were large undertakings involving much labour, and many chosen burial sites developed into cemeteries over generations and centuries. This was also a time when metals and other exotic materials such as amber were traded widely and manufactured into objects of desire in order to impress others and display rank. It is likely that there was much competition between regions to obtain fashionable materials such as gold and amber, and the links between people and communities which underpinned this probably had very deep roots.

Several cups of gold or other precious materials are known from Britain and Europe which date to this period, and some are known to be from burials – Rillaton is one such example. In each case they were just one of a range of fine objects taken out of circulation and buried with an important individual. Whoever was buried at

Ringlemere was therefore probably of high status, although as we know so little about the structure of Bronze Age society we cannot say much more.

Aside from being part of richly furnished burials of important people, how did these cups function in life? Virtually all of them had conical bases, and could not have stood up by themselves. So did they have a stand made out of some perishable material like wood? Or, once filled with drink, were they intended not to be set down until drained? Were they passed around from hand to hand? Once again, we do not know; but we do have plenty of evidence for the importance of ceremonial meals or feasts at various times in prehistory (see also p. 68). These cups might have had an important function on such occasions, and it may be that it was these special occasions, as much as the value attached to the precious cup and its craftsmanship, which determined their importance to these ancient societies. Further research into the cup and the site where it was found might help to answer some of these questions.

Hampshire aristocrats: the Winchester gold

Date of discovery: 2000; date of burial: probably late first century BC

In spring 2000, Sally Worrell received a telephone call from a local detectorist with news of a discovery which would arguably change our view of Iron Age Britain for ever. Sally was at the time the Finds Liaison Officer for Hampshire, a position created as a result of the Portable Antiquities Scheme (see Chapter 1). Like her colleagues in other parts of Britain where the Scheme was also operating at this time, Sally had worked very hard to build bridges with local detectorists, and on that particular day this hard work paid off. The call came from Kevan Halls, a retired local florist who had been metal detecting for a number of years in various parts of the county (fig. 29). Kevan told Sally that he had found a brooch which he thought might be gold, although he was unsure of the date. On seeing the brooch, Sally confirmed that it was gold, and suggested it was Roman or Iron Age. The British Museum was asked to

29 Kevan Halls, the finder of the Winchester gold jewellery.

30 One of the large necklace torcs in the Winchester hoard. The unusually flexible nature of the torc is clear.

identify it – if it were Iron Age, it would be only the third or fourth gold example ever found in Britain. This immediately placed an importance on the discovery even before any further finds had been recovered from the site.

Kevan Halls then returned to the field where the brooch had been located, and was asked to mark the locations of any further finds. He subsequently made an even more spectacular discovery: a necklace or torc of unparalleled type (fig. 30). Kevan went on to find a further three gold brooches and a chain for linking two of the brooches together. He also found another necklace torc, smaller but the same style as the first, under a hedge at the edge of the field. The final parts of the set consisted of two gold ingot bracelets. At an inquest held at Winchester in March 2001, the whole find was declared treasure and was eventually acquired by the British Museum, with Mr Halls and the landowner receiving £350,000 as a Treasure reward. This was the highest reward given to a finder for a discovery since the Treasure Act was introduced in 1997, and reflected the huge importance of this assemblage of material.

The Winchester gold, as it is commonly known, is one of the most unusual sets of Iron Age jewellery found anywhere in western Europe (fig. 31). Although the brooches are of a fairly well-known type fashionable between about 75 and 25 BC, the necklace torcs are completely without parallel. Torcs worn around the neck became common in the late Iron period across Europe. But they were more than simply fashion accessories as they were frequently associated with power and status amongst the ancient peoples of north-west Europe, often called the Celts (although this is a highly problematic term for them[3]). Torcs are mentioned by Roman writers

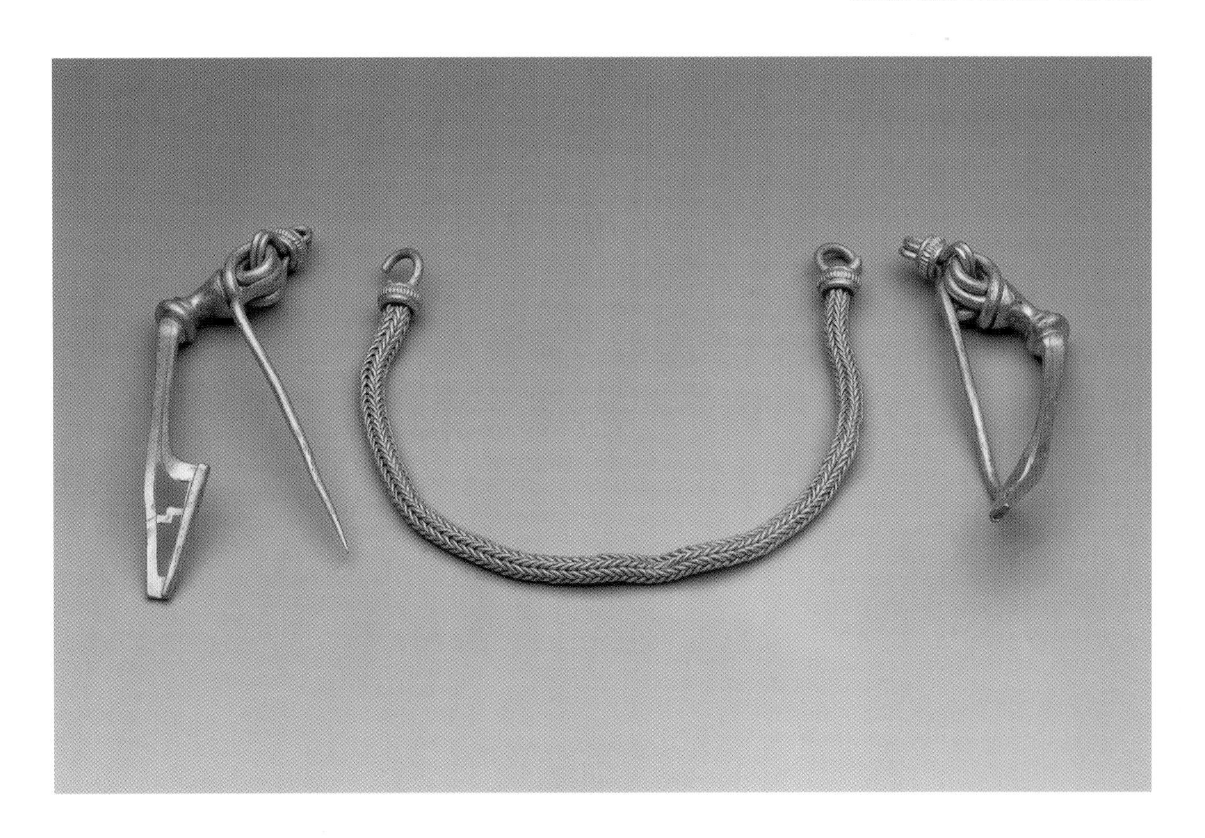

31 *Above* Some of the jewellery from the Winchester hoard – two gold brooches and their link chain.

32 The 'dying Gaul'. This example, a marble copy of a bronze original dating to *c.* 230–220 BC, is in the Capitoline Museum, Rome. An example of a twisted rope-style torc, with the terminals at the front, can be seen around his neck.

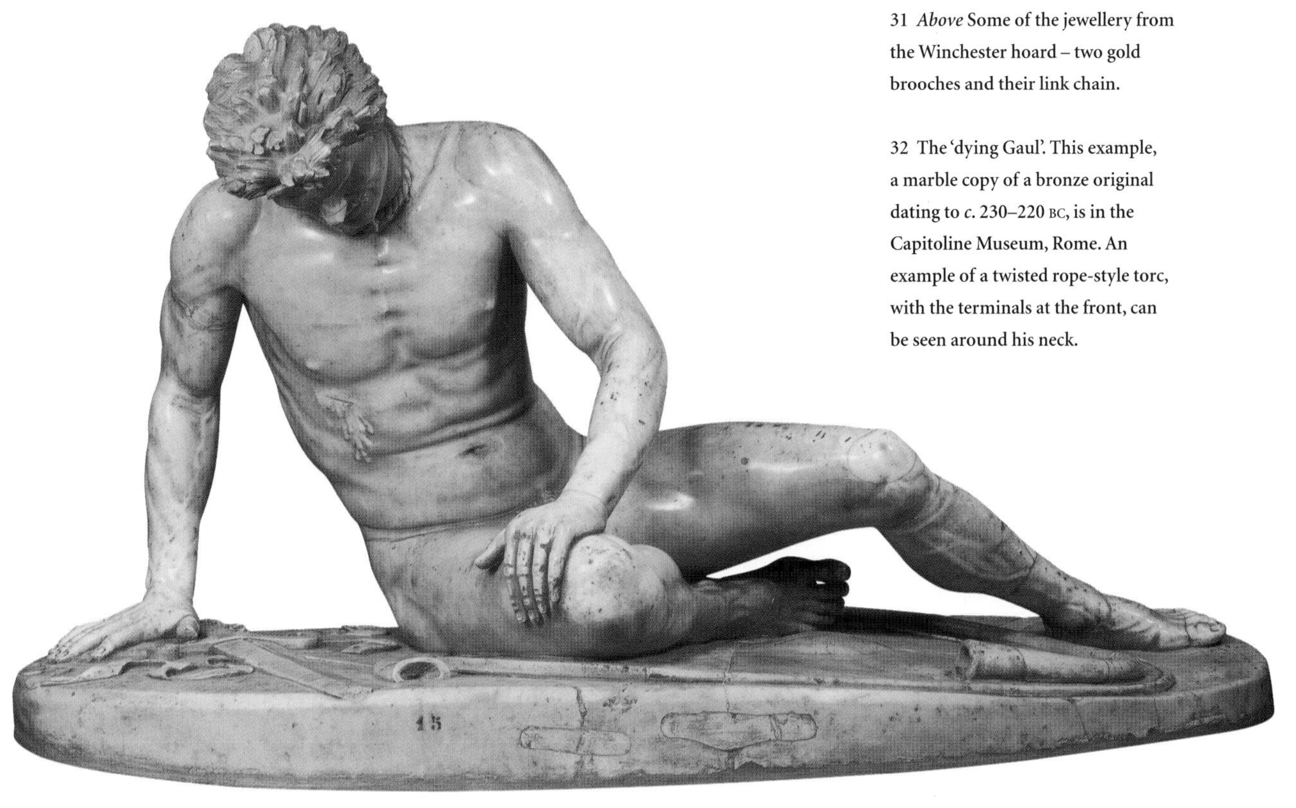

33 An artist's impression of how the Winchester gold jewellery might have been worn.

such as Dio Cassius, who tells us that the famous leader of the Iceni, Boudicca, wore one.[4] Sculpture also shows the torc being worn, the most famous example being the 'dying Gaul', of which a number of Roman copies of a Greek original survive (fig. 32). Torcs, however, seem to have been equally important as ritual objects, often used as offerings to the gods. These types of offerings may account for the series of torc 'nests' buried at Snettisham in Norfolk, one of the most famous late Iron Age sites in western Europe (see p. 137).

The torcs from Winchester, however, were completely different to anything ever discovered before in Britain, or indeed western Europe. Close scientific examination at the British Museum showed that they were made of fine gold wires woven together in a painstaking and extremely skilful manner. This is different to the commonest techniques seen previously in British finds, namely the twisted wire types, in which gold wires are intertwined; and 'loop-in-loop' types, where wires loops are woven together. The Winchester torcs were manufactured in a way which was more common in the Classical world, and seen in jewellery usually found in the Mediterranean region, and even as far from Britain as the Middle East. They also differ from the common British types so far discovered because their terminals could be pinned together. In addition, the technique used to create the torcs made them far more flexible than the rigid torcs usually found. Twisted wire torcs often had to be repaired at the back, as the only way to wear and remove them was to force them on and off the neck by opening and closing them using brute force. The flexibility of the Winchester torcs would have made this unnecessary, and also meant that they would have been very comfortable when worn.

The find seems to have contained two almost complete sets of jewellery. There were two necklace torcs, two sets of brooches, two ingot bracelets, and one link chain to join the brooches together. The other link chain was not discovered despite an extensive search in the area, but would almost certainly have been part of the set. The fact that the necklace torcs are of two different sizes probably means that they belonged to a man and woman. It has been possible to reconstruct the most likely way that the jewellery sets were worn (fig. 33).

So who originally possessed this spectacular jewellery? The owners must have been important individuals to own such stunning objects. As has been seen, the torc was an important status symbol in late Iron Age society, and to own such unusual examples must have marked these individuals out as special – so perhaps they were local aristocrats. The fact that the torcs were made utilising a technique more commonly associated with the Classical world is hugely significant. There are two possible explanations. Firstly, that the craftsman making the torcs may have trained in a workshop somewhere in the Mediterranean and applied his skills back in Britain, perhaps under commission from the original owners. Alternatively, and perhaps more likely, these torcs were acquired from a Roman patron, maybe presented as special gifts. If so, this would show unexpected and unprecedented links between Britain and the Classical world.

But why were the torcs buried? To help answer this question, an archaeological excavation and survey was conducted on the site by Tony Spence and J.D. Hill of the British Museum. This work was inconclusive. It was expected that a burial pit may have been found, and it was even possible that the bones or burnt remains of the owners might have come to light. Neither of these conjectures bore fruit, which suggested to the archaeologists that the jewellery had not been buried with the owners. This might seem disappointing, but in fact is very important contextual evidence. The excavations showed that the jewellery was buried on an exposed hillside in Hampshire away from any settlement. These types of burial are known from other parts of Britain, and a pattern is now beginning to emerge. Other sites on high ground include

the torc burials at Snettisham, Norfolk, already mentioned (see p. 137), as well as new sites such as a series of coin hoards in Leicestershire (see below). Hampshire, however, is an unexpected area for this type of activity, which contributes to making this site so special: although the county has produced sites of Iron Age date, it was not previously known for high-quality metalwork. Taken as a group, these types of burials of precious objects must indicate that a distinctive, probably ritual, practice was taking place amongst communities in different parts of Britain at a broadly similar phase in British prehistory. More research on similar sites will be very important in further understanding them and their place in Iron Age Britain.

Thus the Winchester hoard is a hugely important discovery. But it must not be forgotten that it only came to light through good local relations between an archaeologist and an amateur metal detector user, which provided vital context information for the find. Because the torcs are such unusual objects, if they did not have such a well-established findspot, it would have been extremely difficult to pin down their origins, and they could well have been considered non-British finds. Debate still rages over the exact findspots of other discoveries made in the past, which could have been avoided if the finds had been properly reported in the first instance (see the Mildenhall treasure, p. 171). Such good local relations between amateurs and archaeologists, leading to significant new insights into the period just before the Roman conquest, also underpin the discovery of an equally important and intriguing set of finds in rural Leicestershire.

34 *Left* Excavations at the site of a series of Iron Age coin hoards discovered in east Leicestershire.

Coin hoards in Iron Age Leicestershire

Date of discovery: 2000; date of burial: probably early first century AD

In 2000 a fieldwalker, Ken Wallace, working with a local community archaeology group found a scatter of Roman and Iron Age pottery. He decided to follow up this work with a metal detector scan which began to turn up large numbers of coins on an exposed hillside in rural east Leicestershire (fig. 34). It was soon clear that a site of major importance had been discovered, in which a huge number of Iron Age and early Roman coins were coming to light. (At the time of writing, the exact location of the site cannot be revealed in print because there are concerns that it might be disturbed.) Curators from the British Museum visited the site to offer advice, and English Heritage funded a survey and excavation by the University of Leicester Archaeological Services. The locations of over a dozen coin depositions were identified, and these were lifted in blocks (fig. 35). They were encased in plaster and carefully transported to the British Museum for further analysis by conservators. In the laboratory, X-rays of the blocks were used to guide their excavation and carefully record the positions of the coins and other objects (figs 36–7). This work is ongoing – as the archaeological material emerges, it is cleaned and made available to curators for identification and recording. This process will take many months to complete.

35 A close-up of one of the coin hoards discovered in east Leicestershire. All the hoards were removed in blocks for excavation in the laboratory.

One of the most spectacular blocks included a huge number of coins as well as the remains of a Roman helmet. Although fragmentary, enough survives to tell us that it would have been very elaborate. It is almost certainly a Roman auxiliary parade helmet, probably used by a cavalry officer. It had an iron body completely covered in silver-gilt cladding, with a rich variety of designs. It is an extremely rare discovery and in an unusual context – most military equipment is usually associated with a known Roman military site. Like the Winchester gold (see p. 59), it demonstrates strong links with the Classical world which are somewhat unexpected.

The coins recovered from the Leicestershire site have also proved extremely interesting. The sheer number is currently hard to ascertain exactly, but is certainly in the hundreds and probably the thousands. Some are completely new types (fig. 38). Most can be identified as silver pieces of the Corieltauvi, a tribal group that occupied parts of Leicestershire and Lincolnshire in the late Iron Age and early Roman period, *c.* AD 10–60 (archaeologists sometimes call this the Conquest period). These show an abstract pattern on one side based on a wreath design, and a stylised horse on the other. Sometimes the coins also have unusual inscriptions, such as 'AVN CO', 'IAT ISO', or 'VEPO' (fig. 39), the meanings of which are not entirely clear. They might be the names of important individuals who made the coins, or the places where they were minted.

37 An X-ray of one of the soil blocks removed from the site in east Leicestershire. The large numbers of coins in the soil are clearly visible.

36 *Below* British Museum conservator Marilyn Hockey working on one of the soil blocks from east Leicestershire. Some of the coins are visible on the surface.

38 *Left* Two gold quarter staters from the east Leicestershire site. The coin on the right is particularly interesting as it is the first recorded example of its type. On one side it has the letters 'CVNO', short for Cunobelin, with an ear of corn; on the other, a horse with the letters 'DVBN' below. This may provide a previously unknown link between Cunobelin and someone probably called Dubnovellaunus, other coins of whom are also known.

39 *Above* Iron Age silver coins typical of the Corieltauvi tribe, thousands of which were found at the Leicestershire site.

40 A silver Roman Republican coin with a serrated edge (*denarius serratus*) from the Leicestershire site, minted in Rome *c.* 64 BC. It is one of a number of such coins found at the site and might indicate strong links with Rome long before the invasion by Claudius in AD 43.

Also in the find were gold coins which are a little easier to interpret. These have the letters 'CAMV' on one side and 'CVNO' on the other, the former an abbreviation of the mint name Camulodunum (modern Colchester in Essex), the latter of Cunobelin, referred to by the Roman writer Suetonius as '*Britannorum Rex*' ('King of the Britons'). Cunobelin was probably not the king of the whole of Britain, but certainly had major influence over much of the south during this period. The discovery of his coins in the Midlands suggests his influence was wider than was previously thought.[5] One of the coins, with the name 'CVNO' on one side, is particularly remarkable (see fig. 38). Other coins from the site are Republican denarii which were mainly minted in Rome and could conceivably have found their way to Britain by means of trade and payments, perhaps for mercenaries involved in the Gallic Wars with Julius Caesar (fig. 40). But this is a matter of conjecture, because there is no hard evidence that these particular coins arrived in Britain before the Roman invasion of AD 43.

The site in Leicestershire is extraordinary for a number of reasons. Firstly, the manner of discovery makes it very important – it is a wonderful example of the enthusiasm of amateur fieldwalkers and detectorists, who give up their spare time to understand the archaeology of their local area, and work alongside professional

41 Some coins from the Cunetio hoard, Wiltshire, third century AD, the largest hoard of Roman coins ever found on British soil.

archaeologists and museum curators. Secondly, the site itself is completely unparalleled in the county of Leicestershire and arguably the country as a whole. It is the largest group of Iron Age coins ever discovered in this part of Britain, and the first time that such a group has been excavated *in situ*, having escaped serious disturbance by cultivation over the last 2,000 years. Recently, archaeologists have extended the excavations which have revealed a different type of evidence to the coin hoards: a series of shallow pits full of animal bones, including some complete skulls and carcasses.

But what was the purpose of the Leicestershire site? Although more excavation work and analysis of the finds will be needed, some preliminary ideas can be floated. It seems to have been a ritual meeting ground on a prominent hilltop, and evidence from animal bones found at the site suggests it was also used for feasting. The coin hoards and other objects such as the Roman helmet seem to have been offerings – another part of ritual activities. The animal bones also seem to have been buried in a deliberate way which may mean that, in addition to feasting, animal sacrifice was taking place. The people at these ceremonies probably came from the tribal area we generally ascribe to the Corieltauvi, and they may have come from miles around to attend. The site seems to have been in use in the early part of the first century AD; it was abandoned soon after, certainly by the late first century AD. Alongside other new Iron Age discoveries such as Winchester (see p. 59) and older sites such as Snettisham (see p. 137), the Leicestershire deposits will undoubtedly transform our picture of a remarkable period in Britain – the end of prehistory and the beginning of Roman rule.

Treasures from Roman Britain

The arrival of the Romans in AD 43 did not suddenly cause every aspect of life in Britain to change. It is a popular misconception that the people of Britain suddenly became 'Roman' – toga-wearing, Latin-speaking, tax-paying citizens – as opposed to a bunch of unruly, uncivilised barbarians.

The treasure finds of prehistoric date already discussed in this chapter are one way in which this picture is shown to be wrong. Instead they portray a complex, intricate society with a diverse range of self-expression, from the manufacture and use of sophisticated gold objects to complex rituals of death and burial. When the Romans arrived, the material culture certainly changed as new ideas and ways of living were introduced, but the people using them were just the same as before – equally complex and sophisticated. Three major treasure finds, all of the late Roman period, provide illustrations of why this was the case.

Pots of cash: the Cunetio hoard

Date of discovery: 1978; date of burial: after AD 274 (late third century AD)

The Cunetio hoard is the largest single group of Roman coins ever unearthed from British soil (fig. 41).[6] Over 2,000 coin hoards of Roman date are known from Britain, but few come near to matching its size.[7] Cunetio was the name of a small Roman settlement roughly halfway between Aquae Sulis (modern Bath) and Calleva (modern Silchester), just outside the village of Mildenhall in Wiltshire. The hoard was discovered in 1978 by two metal detectorists, and consists of around 54,000 Roman coins mostly dating to the third century AD, which had been buried in a large storage jar (fig. 42) and a lead box. Its sheer size makes it one of the most important treasures ever found in Britain, but it is much more than the sum of its parts – its contents reflect a very troubled and eventful time in the history of the Roman Empire, and show how Britain, as a province on the northern edge, was affected by these wider events.

42 The large storage jar from Cunetio, Wiltshire, in which most of the hoard had been secreted.

The third century AD is often regarded as the time from which the Roman Empire began to go into decline. None of the emperors seemed capable of holding together what was now a vast empire, stretching from Spain in the west to Syria in the east. Ancient writers tell of major barbarian attacks on a number of fronts, in particular the frontier created by the Rhine and Danube rivers in central Europe, and the eastern frontier with the Parthian Empire of Iran. By the late third century in the west, the situation had deteriorated to the extent that a breakaway 'empire' under Postumus (AD 260–69) and his successors was formed, covering the Roman provinces of Gaul, Spain, Britain and Germany. The Gallic Empire, as it is known, showed that there was little confidence in Rome's ability to protect the northern frontiers from attack. As a result, certain legions in the Roman army took matters into their own hands and declared different generals as emperor. These unofficial emperors are often called usurpers.

The coinage in the Cunetio treasure reflects this chaotic situation because it contains a mixture of coins struck by a number of these different individuals (fig. 43). Many were made by official emperors such as Gallienus (AD 253–68), most at mints in the heart of the Roman Empire, at Rome itself and at Milan in northern Italy. The treasure also contains coins of usurpers such as Tetricus (AD 271–4). His coins were struck at two mints in Gaul (modern France) – the heartland of the breakaway Gallic Empire – although we do not know exactly where they were located.

Both Gallienus and Tetricus principally struck coins to pay their troops and staff. Coins were a very important way of ensuring that the army and civil service stayed loyal, simply because the payment kept them contented as they were in turn able to support themselves and their families. Therefore, for would-be emperors such as Tetricus, it was vital that they had coins struck in order to keep their own men satisfied. This is why new mints were set up in Gaul by Postumus – the first Gallic emperor – to rival those of Rome.

Despite the fact that two different sets of coins were being issued for emperors and usurpers, they look very similar. All are known as 'radiates' because they show the emperor's head with a crown of sun's rays. They are also a low value coinage, largely consisting of base metal such as copper, with a small quantity of silver – only 2 per cent by the AD 270s. Both types show the emperor bearded, and often looking rather rugged, probably because most of them were tough military generals. The Gallic emperors also copied the legends of the official emperors, but substituted their own names. So 'GALLIENVS AVG' is replaced by 'TETRICVS AVG', as both were claiming to be emperor ('AVG' is an abbreviation of 'Augustus' or 'emperor'). This demonstrates how coins were also used for propaganda. By calling themselves 'Augustus' on their coins, they were asserting their authority – even though in actuality this meant they only governed some provinces in the west, not the whole of the Roman Empire.

The Cunetio hoard also contains a number of copies of both official and Gallic Empire coins. These were probably made in Britain and are often called 'barbarous radiates'. They can be recognised by the fact that they are rather irregular in appearance – the emperor's head might have features which are not quite in the right places or which are the wrong size, and the letters in the inscriptions can be unevenly spaced and even garbled. Why these copies were made is not entirely clear. They might suggest that official coinage issues were in short supply. As has already been stated, official coins were principally struck to pay the army and civil service. In using these payments to buy goods and services, the coins then filtered down to the civilian population, who in turn would use them for the same reasons and to pay their taxes. But if the supply of official coins dried up, the civilian population had little coinage available to use on a daily basis. So copies might have been produced in order that the wheels of the economy could continue to turn. This shows that people were more reliant on money, and particularly small change, than we might expect of a society from such a

43 Obverse and reverse of three coins from Cunetio, Wiltshire. These include official issues of the emperor Gallienus (top left, upper and lower shots), the Gallic Empire usurper Postumus (top right, upper and lower), and a locally produced poor quality copy or 'barbarous radiate' (bottom coin, upper and lower).

distant age. Alternatively, copying could have been simple fraud – counterfeit coinage produced to be passed off as the real thing.

Thus, the coins in the Cunetio hoard mirror both political and economic events of the third century AD. But who might have owned this vast quantity of coins and why was it buried? The first stage in trying to answer these questions is to look at when the hoard was gathered. The latest coins date to about AD 274 which means that the hoard must have been buried soon after this date, within the next few years at most. And the majority of the coins in the find span a period of about twenty years, although there are some earlier pieces. This suggests that it was put together over the period of somebody's adult lifetime, rather than a short period of one or two years, in which case we would expect the coins to date to a shorter period, perhaps only a few years. Maybe this suggests that the owner of the Cunetio hoard was a local businessman or woman who was enormously successful and was able to amass these coins during their working life.

This leaves the other question of why were the coins buried. In the Roman period, Cunetio was a small rural settlement which probably began life as a military fort. At the time of the burial, the town was a civilian settlement surrounded by a defensive ditch. The coins were placed outside these defences in a massive storage jar, over half a metre in height, which would originally have contained foodstuffs. The whole jar was placed at the bottom of a deep pit, the right way up. Other fragments of large storage vessels were also found in the area nearby. This suggests that it may have already been an area where food was stored. In the Roman period, large storage jars were often sunk into the ground to keep their contents cool and fresh, and often a whole series of these jars is found together, as a Roman equivalent of a household larder. Therefore, perhaps the owner was using the storage jar as a hiding place for his or her coins, with the general storage area perceived to be a good decoy – others would think it was just for food. Later, a lead box containing thousands more coins was buried with the jar. Unfortunately, however, these were not kept separate from the rest of the coins by the finder when excavated – if they had been, we might have understood them better.

The above tale of a local businessman or woman perhaps taking advantage of the location of Cunetio as an important point in south-west Britain for trade, and becoming rich in the process, is attractive but will never be provable. Nevertheless, whoever did put the hoard together had managed to gather the largest single group of Roman coins ever discovered in Britain. Although most are of low intrinsic value, as a group it represents over 22 kilograms of silver – a sizeable quantity of precious metal for one person to amass. Clearly the owner never returned to retrieve this wealth, perhaps getting caught up in the events of this turbulent time; and the location of the deposit remained unknown until just over 1,700 years had passed.

The Mildenhall treasure

Date of discovery: 1942; date of burial: late fourth century AD

At the height of the Second World War, life in Suffolk carried on largely unaffected by outside events. Like much of rural England, Suffolk farms were essential to the maintenance of domestic food supplies, with all resources from Britain, both human and material, being channelled into the war effort.

Gordon Butcher, like any other Suffolk farmer, was exempt from military duty because of his importance to agriculture. In January 1942 he set out as normal to plough some land for a man called Rolfe at West Row, Mildenhall. Butcher's work started normally, as he methodically ploughed evenly spaced deep furrows in the soil. Late that morning, however, Butcher's plough suddenly stopped as it struck a large obstacle in the ground. This was a not entirely unprecedented occurrence: occasionally buried oaks snagged ploughs and caused them to break from the tractor. But Butcher had not struck a buried oak: he had discovered one of the most important treasures of Roman silver ever found in the Roman Empire, subsequently known as the Mildenhall treasure. It is on display today in the British Museum, where it forms a cornerstone of the Romano-British collections, and is an essential element in the story of Roman Britain and indeed the Roman Empire as a whole.

The story of the following events is recounted in a short story by Roald Dahl which first appeared in Britain in a collection of Dahl's short stories in 1977, and has since been republished with evocative illustrations by Ralph Steadman.[8] This story was one of the main reasons I myself became interested in the past, and I would never have dreamed when I first read it that I might one day be in charge of curating the Mildenhall treasure! As Dahl recounts, the hoard of thirty-four pieces of silver plate was dug up by Butcher and his boss Sidney Ford, although it was Ford who took the pieces home and spent the rest of the war cleaning the find. When he had finished, he proudly displayed the treasure on two sideboards in his house (fig. 44); his grandson remembers the Great Dish being used at Christmas as a fruit bowl.[9] The treasure only became known in 1946, when an amateur antiquarian, Dr Hugh Fawcett, visited Ford and saw some of the items in the find which he immediately recognised as being silver. Fawcett persuaded Ford to send some of the pieces to the British Museum for scientific analysis, which confirmed that the metal was silver. Ford somewhat reluctantly reported the find (see p. 45) to his local police station in Mildenhall, and the police then seized it. At a Treasure Trove inquest in 1946, Ford maintained that he believed that the pieces were made of pewter, and thus did not require reporting. The coroner decided that both Ford and Butcher should receive an award of £1,000 each – far less than the true value of the material – because an attempt had clearly been made to conceal the discovery and the coroner felt the reward should reflect this. The silver was acquired by the British Museum soon after.

44 This photograph, taken some time between 1942 and 1946, shows some of the Mildenhall treasure sitting on a sideboard in Sidney Ford's house. Visible are the Great Dish, flanked by the Bacchic platters and the smallest flanged bowls.

45 The Mildenhall treasure, Suffolk. Roman silver tableware mainly of the fourth century AD.

The story, however, does not end there, and there is still much to be done to understand the true significance of the discovery. Some of the silver was still tarnished when it came to the Museum, and the plough had damaged some of the pieces. Therefore the conservation department spent a number of months cleaning and consolidating the silver to restore it to its former glory. The treasure was promptly published in a short guide,[10] and then re-published thirty years later in a fuller catalogue.[11]

The Mildenhall treasure is a magnificent example of late Roman craftsmanship (fig. 45). Most of the pieces were made in the fourth century AD, and at least one piece – the covered bowl – was made rather earlier, in the third century AD. The style of some of the items is coherent, for example the Great Dish and the Bacchic platters, which tells us that they were almost certainly made as a group in one workshop. Other items, such as the niello dish, are very different in character, which may imply another place of origin.

It is by no means clear where these silversmith workshops were located. At this time, the Roman Empire had a number of important centres at which the emperor's court was sometimes located: not just Rome in the west and Constantinople (modern Istanbul) in the east, but other places such as Antioch, Trier, Milan and Ravenna. All these places may have been using silver plate for gifts as part of the workings of the imperial court, for example to bestow imperial patronage on others, but that does not

necessarily mean that silver plate was made there. However, we do know that at this period silver coinage was controlled through a series of imperial mints, and the coinages produced bear mint marks telling us where they originated. For Britain, these mints included Lyon in France and Trier in Germany. It is not inconceivable that the production of silver and gold coinage was also related to the production of silver plate, and that workshops could have been located in the same places. From what we know of the manufacture of precious metal items in the fourth century, it is therefore unlikely that these pieces were produced locally near Mildenhall.

As for how the Mildenhall treasure was made, the best evidence comes from an analysis of the Great Dish which was carried out during the 1970s by the British Museum's Department of Scientific Research. Many people assume that the dish was cast in a mould, but this is not the case. Instead, a large piece of silver weighing over 8 kilograms was 'raised' on an anvil. This means that different hammers were used to beat the vessel into the shape we see today. The most likely method used to decorate it is known as 'chasing'. This would have involved using a series of small hammers and punches from the front to form the outlines of the figures and other decoration (unlike the 'repoussé' technique, where hammering occurs from the back). In addition, some decoration was achieved by using engraving tools, particularly for some of the 'background' decoration such as the parts of Pan's cloak behind his arm. The beaded rim would then have been created using a series of special punches. Finally, using a lathe, all of the surfaces, front and back, were smoothed by scraping, and the whole of the surface design was then burnished.

The designs on the pieces are mainly Classical in style. The Great Dish (fig. 46) shows a head of Oceanus in the centre, and then has two other friezes of decoration, with the innermost showing a sea revel of Nereids and sea creatures, and the outermost a drinking contest between the Greek hero Heracles and the Roman god of wine, Bacchus. The Bacchic theme is continued on two smaller platters, and many other vessels have similar designs drawn from the Classical arena. The influence of Christianity, as on the Hoxne hoard (see p. 78), is also present in the find in the form of Chi-Rho monograms on some of the spoons. This symbol, which combines the first two letters of Christ's name in Greek, is also accompanied by an alpha and an omega, the first and last letters of the Greek alphabet (as in 'I am the beginning and the end'). These devices encapsulate the changing world in which the owners of the treasure lived. Old pagan, Classical beliefs were still strongly felt and formed much of the stock of late Roman artistic endeavour, but new Christian symbols and allegorical themes were beginning to appear, both on metal vessels and in other media such as mosaics, wall paintings and illuminated manuscripts.

Although the artistic brilliance of the silver pieces in the Mildenhall treasure is beyond dispute, much still needs to be understood about how it fits into the wider context of the late Roman world. In the immediate aftermath of its discovery, some archaeologists were doubtful that it had even been found at Mildenhall at all. Britain

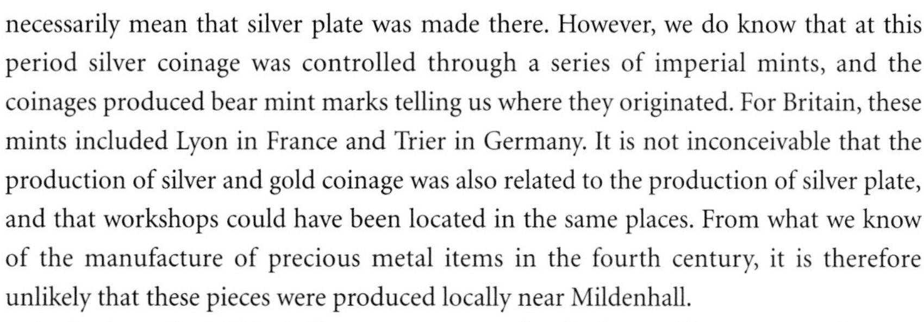

46 The Great Dish from the Mildenhall treasure, the most magnificent piece in the assemblage.

as a Roman province was viewed as being something of a cultural backwater: the richness of the remains of the Mediterranean parts of the Roman Empire gave British archaeologists something of an inferiority complex. Conspiracy theories began to develop, the most popular being the possibility that the Americans had flown the treasure into the airbase at Mildenhall from North Africa. As already explained, most of the pieces were probably made in a Mediterranean workshop, and thus the doubters thought that it was likely to have belonged to someone there, perhaps the occupants of a villa estate in Tunisia or Morocco. Further doubts were cast because

two archaeologists, Gordon Fowler and Tom Lethbridge, failed to find any further pieces, or the supposed location of the pit in which the pieces had been originally buried, when they conducted some survey and excavation in 1947 (fig. 47).

The North Africa theory is not credible, as the airbase was not used by the Americans until after the war; and it seems that Fowler and Lethbridge were probably looking in the wrong place, either because Ford, who was asked to lead them to the spot, deliberately misled them, or because after five years no traces of the original burial site were visible anyway. So there is no strong reason to believe that the treasure was not found at Mildenhall. Subsequent discoveries of other treasures in East Anglia – such as that found at nearby Hoxne (see p. 78) – show us that Britain was not a poor province of the Roman Empire as many people once thought.

MILDENHALL: DISPLAY SILVER OR OPULENT DINING WARE?

The other aspect of the Mildenhall treasure which vexes archaeologists is how it was used by its owners, and indeed who the owners were. In the British Museum, the treasure is displayed so that we can properly appreciate the richness of the designs and the sublime imagery. But in the past, we cannot be certain that it would have been displayed purely as a work of art – it may also have functioned as a dining service. It should also be remembered that its imagery did not benefit from modern bright artificial lights – light levels indoors in the Roman period would always have been fairly low. Candles and lamps were the only source of artificial light, which may have produced a rather eerie effect as the light flittered erratically across the surfaces of the pieces, but would never have provided enough light for the items to be appreciated fully.

All the items in the treasure could have served a practical function as dining vessels, perhaps when the owners were entertaining guests and sought to impress them. Dining in the Roman period was very different from today, with guests usually reclining on couches, rather than sitting around a table, and plates of food shared buffet-style. Servants may have provided guests with smaller plates from which to dine, and for special meals there would have been more courses than nowadays. These types of dining scene, although fairly common on art of the early empire from sites like Pompeii, are extremely rare in the art of the late Roman world, so we do not have much evidence about the practicalities of mealtimes. Some mosaics from North Africa show scenes of outdoor dining broadly contemporary with the Mildenhall treasure, and in a warm Mediterranean climate eating *al fresco* as today was undoubtedly common. But it is much harder to imagine a family in rural Suffolk, which would have most of the time been rather cold and wet, spending their leisure time entertaining guests with impressive banquets taken from silver dishes, and even harder to imagine this occurring outside.

47 Archaeologists Gordon Fowler and Tom Lethbridge attempting to find the site where the Mildenhall treasure had been buried. Note the use of a primitive metal detector. Fowler and Lethbridge grew suspicious about whether this was the findspot after they failed to locate any evidence for the supposed burial.

However, there is a very useful illustration in the form of a page from an illuminated manuscript from the *Vergilius Romanus*, a fourth- to fifth-century work kept in the Vatican Museums (fig. 48). Some believe that this manuscript originated in Britain, so it may even have direct relevance to daily life in the province itself. The illumination shows three diners[12] reclining on a *stibadium*, a curved couch favoured in the late empire. In the centre of the diners is a large platter with a fish on it – the platter is not unlike the large niello plate in the Mildenhall treasure, as the rim appears to be beaded, although it is oval in shape. Also similar to some vessels in the treasure are three small flanged bowls placed around the plate as individual serving vessels, perhaps for soup or some other kind of liquid foodstuff. Wine is being served by a servant holding a ewer and being drunk by the guests from glass beakers, and another servant holds a second ewer containing water, and a *patera* (handled dish). Ewers are not present in the Mildenhall assemblage, but at nearby Hoxne (see p. 78), the handle of such a ewer was discovered amongst the hoard. Interestingly, at Burgh Castle in Norfolk, some examples of the conical glass drinking beakers, similar to those shown in this illustration, were discovered.

It is perfectly reasonable, therefore, to suggest that the Mildenhall treasure may have been used for opulent dining, rather than just for show. But however it was used during its lifetime, it is undoubtedly one of the most magnificent sets of late Roman silverware to survive into modern times, and continues to provide huge fascination year on year for the millions of visitors to the British Museum.

A real-life treasure chest: the Hoxne hoard

Date of discovery: 1992; date of burial: c. *AD 410–30*

Eric Lawes's fifteen minutes of fame came in 1992 when he discovered, with the aid of a metal detector, the largest hoard of Roman gold and silver ever found on British soil. The discovery even made its way on to the front page of the *Sun* (fig. 49)! The most important element of the story of Hoxne's discovery is that we know so much about where and how it was buried. This is very rare for finds of treasure. Mildenhall, of a similar date to Hoxne, typifies this problem – we will probably never know exactly where it had been secreted (see p. 76), with at least six different locations offered by the finders.

Mr Lawes's amazing story begins with his search for a hammer which had been lost in a field near the village of Hoxne, Suffolk. After receiving a strong signal from his metal detector, he began to dig. But, instead of the lost hammer (which was found later), he began to uncover large numbers of gold and silver coins, and items of gold jewellery, including a body chain (figs 50–51). What Mr Lawes did next, however, is the pivotal point in the story. Having removed hundreds of items, particularly coins, from the soil, and realising that there were many more finds to be made, he stopped digging and decided to call in the experts. He contacted the Suffolk Archaeological Unit, who were soon out on site. They were able to excavate the rest of the hoard, and record the exact positions of the objects in the ground, and how they related to each other. They were also able to trace the outlines of a wooden chest in which the treasure had been placed, some remains of which had

48 An illumination from the *Vergilius Romanus*, a fourth-century AD manuscript. The scene, which shows three diners reclining on a curved couch (*stibadium*), includes silver vessels not unlike some of those in the Mildenhall treasure.

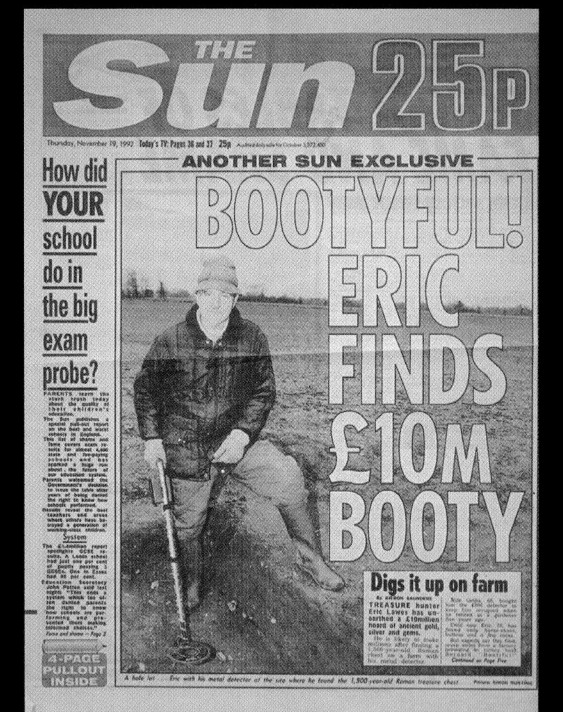

THE Sun 25p

Thursday, November 19, 1992 Today's TV: Pages 36 and 37 25p

How did YOUR school do in the big exam probe?

PARENTS learn the stark truth today about the quality of their children's education.

System

Fame and shame — Page 2

4-PAGE PULLOUT INSIDE

ANOTHER SUN EXCLUSIVE

BOOTYFUL! ERIC FINDS £10M BOOTY

Digs it up on farm

TREASURE hunter Eric Lawes has unearthed a £10million hoard of ancient gold, silver and gems.

Continued on Page Five

A hole lot ... Eric with his metal detector at the site where he found the 1,500-year-old Roman treasure chest

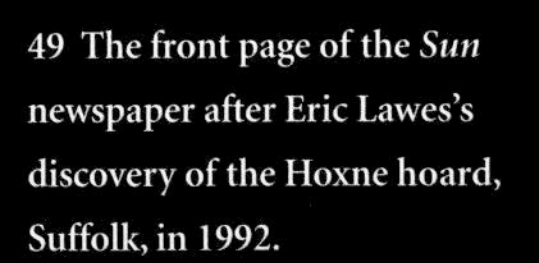

49 The front page of the *Sun* newspaper after Eric Lawes's discovery of the Hoxne hoard, Suffolk, in 1992.

50 Eric Lawes, the finder of the Hoxne hoard, with the body chain, the finest item of gold jewellery in the find.

51 The gold body chain from the Hoxne hoard as it would have been worn. The size of the body chain suggests that its female owner must have been very petite.

survived (see p. 84). This type of work is very skilled and requires years of experience – archaeologists are able to notice subtle details in the soil which the untrained eye can easily miss.

After excavation, the whole assemblage was taken to the British Museum where it could be properly studied. With the help of his wife, Mr Lawes had washed some of the finds in the kitchen sink on the day that he had made his discovery. This cannot be considered best practice as much important information can be lost by cleaning archaeological metalwork in this way, but as most of the finds were gold and silver

54 *Right* Three pepperpots (*piperatoria*) from the Hoxne hoard. All are exquisitely made and decorated – the central one is the so-called 'Empress' pepperpot, which is in the form of a bust of a late Roman woman.

52 A stack of bracelets from the Hoxne treasure being removed from the ground by the Suffolk Archaeological Unit. When they were carefully excavated back at the British Museum, it became clear that they had been forced together in order to save space.

53 A stack of spoons from the Hoxne treasure just after excavation. The fact that the spoons were stacked tells us that the owners took a great deal of care with the burial.

coins, not too much damage was done. Thankfully, however, the rest of the finds were kept with their surrounding soil intact because they had been excavated professionally.

Back at the British Museum, careful cleaning and conservation work took a number of weeks to complete and threw up some extremely interesting information about how the treasure had been buried. Inside a large wooden chest objects had been carefully stacked in groups, for example sets of spoons of similar type (fig. 53). Hay had been used to protect some of these stacked objects, for instance a set of five silver bowls. Some objects had been placed inside textile bags, with some traces of textile still surviving – on most archaeological sites these would have long since perished. So even at this early stage, it was clear that the people burying the find had taken a great deal of care – they had not just randomly filled the chest and stashed it in a large hole.

Once cleaned, it was possible to begin working out exactly what made up the treasure, which was the job of a number of museum specialists. The hoard consists of over 15,000 late Roman silver coins, known as *siliquae* and *miliarenses*, and around 560 gold coins known as *solidi*. All the coins are of exceptionally high quality, well struck and with a high precious metal content – a far cry from the rather poor coins from finds such as the Cunetio hoard (see p. 69). A large proportion have been 'clipped', which means that their edges were snipped off, probably a number of years after they were originally struck. The clippings were then likely to have been used to make copies of the official coinage issues, of which the hoard contains a number. The treasure also includes superb gold jewellery, consisting of body chains, bracelets (fig. 52) and finger-rings, some of which were inscribed with personal names such as 'Juliana'. There is also silver tableware in the form of bowls, spoons, ladles and wine

EXERCITVS

The making of the Hoxne treasure chest

The Hoxne find fits neatly into the popular perception of treasure – a sizeable quantity of gold and silver buried in a large wooden chest. For the 'Treasure: Finding our Past' exhibition, it was therefore decided to follow up this image of a quintessential 'treasure chest' by making a reconstruction of it. There were, of course, also good archaeological reasons for doing this. At the time of discovery, a number of traces of the box survived, but it was unclear how these different elements fitted together, and a reconstruction supervised by a team of experts would help to solve this (fig. 56).

Deciding how the chest should look was no easy task, as the wooden remains of the original chest had long since perished. But on discovery, the archaeologists who excavated the treasure were able to establish important clues as to what the chest would have originally looked like and how the pieces had been placed in it. The chest had left a distinctive soil mark in the ground, which archaeologists were able to see when the treasure was excavated. This enabled the team to work out the rough size of the whole chest. In any case, the objects had not moved very much from their original positions, which meant that the edges of the chest could also be surmised from the locations of the outermost treasure items. It was also possible to estimate the depth of the chest in the same manner.

Having established the size of the chest, it was then necessary to work out how it might have appeared. Much of this work has come from looking at other sources of evidence for wooden chests of the Roman period. One such chest was found near Milton Keynes, Buckinghamshire, in 1976,[13] and this well-preserved example provided some clues as to the original appearance of the Hoxne chest. The joints of the Milton Keynes chest were of 'dovetail' type, and iron nails had been used to attach the bottom of the chest to the sides. In addition, the lid had been fitted with two hinges, and iron straps had been added to give the chest further strength. Although the hinges and joints on the Hoxne chest did not survive, iron nails and straps were also found, so it was decided to model the reconstruction along similar lines to that found at Milton Keynes.

56 Making a reconstruction of the chest in which the Hoxne hoard was buried. The team of experts included Teresa Rumble, 3-D designer; Roy Mandeville from Plowden Smith, the company responsible for making the chest (centre); Richard Hobbs, British Museum curator (left); and Hayley Bullock, British Museum conservator (right). Other members of the team were Catherine Johns who is publishing the non-coin elements of the hoard, and Jude Plouviez of Suffolk County Council, one of the archaeologists who excavated the find.

The Hoxne chest also contained at least three other smaller caskets. Evidence for these was discovered in the form of delicate bone and wood inlays from one casket, and small silver fittings, including two silver padlocks and decorative silver rosettes, for two other boxes. One of the padlocks still had the remains of a leather backing, so we also know that one of these smaller caskets had a thin leather wrapping.

All this information was needed to make the outer chest. It was also decided that two of the inner caskets would be made, but this required more guesswork as their dimensions were not as clear as the larger outer chest. Clear acrylic ('Perspex'), was used to make both the chest and the inner caskets. Shelves were added in order to place objects at the appropriate levels. These would not have been present in the original chest, but were necessary for the reconstruction, as only samples of the different types of item in the treasure, not the whole find, were being used for the exhibition. Pieces of 'frosted' (opaque) acrylic were used to mimic chest fittings.

As for the positions of the objects, plans made by the archaeologists excavating the hoard and work by the conservators at the British Museum gave a good idea of where the items had been placed (fig. 57). A larger casket (fig. 58), probably with the bone and wooden inlay, had been put at the bottom of the outer chest. Inside this casket was placed a number of items, including the small silver jugs, the silver tigress ewer handle, a stack of ladles and the empress pepper pot. Another stack of long-handled spoons was placed at the bottom of the large chest around the sides of this casket. Leant against the side of the box was a stack of gold bracelets. These had been quite roughly treated, as they had been rammed into the middle of a heavy gold armlet. A set of four silver bowls had been carefully stacked and placed upside down in a silver dish. Hay was used to separate these bowls. The whole set had then been placed on its side against one of the walls of the chest.

More stacks of spoons and ladles had been placed at the top of the box. The huge quantities of coins, probably in cloth bags, had also been placed to fill in any remaining gaps, and others might have simply been poured in. Unfortunately we do not know if the gold coins were kept separate from the silver ones, or if there were any other distinct groups – this might have helped in understanding more about the coinage of the time. As a last act, the gold body chains, necklaces and finger-rings were placed right at the top of the box, probably wrapped in another piece of cloth.

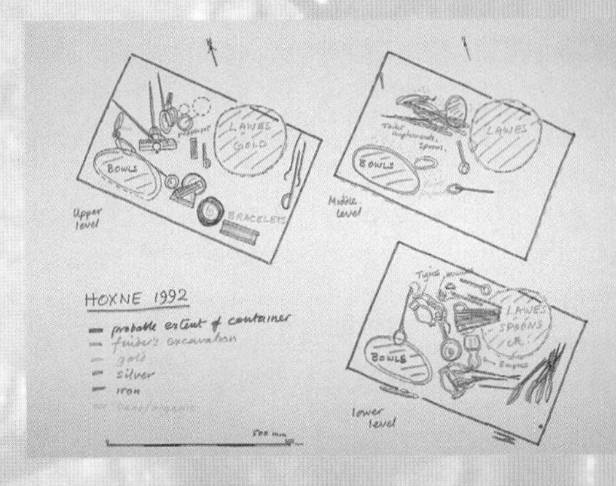

57 *Above* Three sketch plans of how the objects in the Hoxne treasure lay in the ground when excavated. These plans were important for understanding how the different elements of the hoard had been positioned inside the wooden chest.

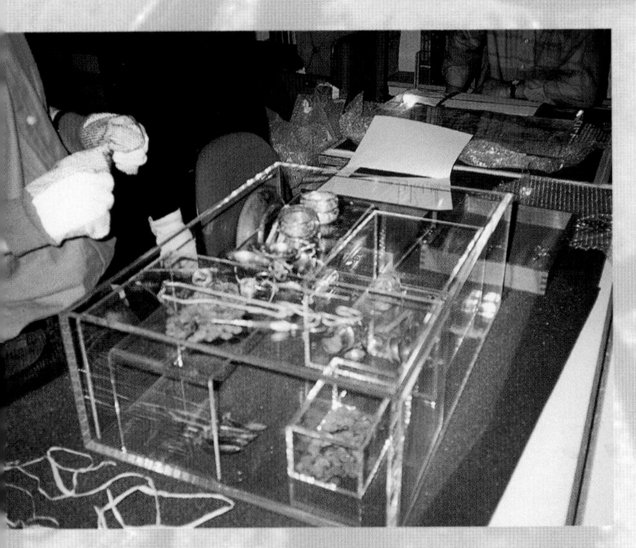

58 The reconstruction of the Hoxne chest.

strainers. In addition, there are ornate and unusual tableware items such as pepper-pots (fig. 54), including one in the form of the bust of a lady, and the handle of a ewer (wine jug) in the form of a tigress. The latter two objects are perhaps the most eye-catching in the treasure. Other precious objects include two small silver jugs and a number of silver toothpicks.[14]

The coins in the Hoxne hoard are extremely important for dating the whole find (fig. 55). Fifteen different Roman emperors are represented, with the oldest coin minted by Constantine II (AD 337–40), one of Constantine the Great's sons. The latest coins in the hoard date to the time of Constantine III, a military general who was declared emperor in Britain in AD 407, and who controlled parts of nearby provinces (mainly Gaul (modern France) and Iberia (modern Spain and Portugal)) until his death in AD 411. The other gold and silver objects were made at about the same time as the coins. This means that the treasure must have been buried some time after that date, probably in the AD 420s or 430s.

The sheer size of the Hoxne treasure is quite exceptional. It contains more than 3.5 kilograms of gold and almost 25 kilograms of silver. After it was declared Treasure Trove, Mr Lawes received £1.75 million as a reward, one of the largest payments ever made to a finder. But it is Hoxne's historical and archaeological significance which is far more important than its financial value. Research on the finds themselves has been continuing ever since it was acquired by the British Museum, the results of which are soon to be published.[15]

Why were the Mildenhall and Hoxne treasures buried?

Both the Mildenhall and Hoxne treasures were buried at the end of the fourth or early in the fifth century AD. Many view this as a time of major upheaval in British history. But the details of what was going on at this time are extremely uncertain and there is very little reliable written historical information: for this reason, it is often referred to as the 'Dark Ages'. We are largely dependent upon people commenting on this period from a distance, either because they were writing at a later date, or because they lived somewhere other than Britain. None of these writers thus provide first-hand accounts. This is why archaeological discoveries dating to this time which shed some light on this period are of such importance. Mildenhall and Hoxne are just such finds, so what do they tell us?

Firstly, they tell us something about society. All the objects in both finds are made of precious metals, and many are of exceptional workmanship, for example the Great Dish in Mildenhall or the pepper pots in Hoxne. So they must have belonged to people at the upper end of society – they were not the sorts of objects which featured in most people's everyday lives. Unfortunately, we do not know who these people were, even though we have some of their names ('Juliana' and 'Ursicinus' in Hoxne, 'Pascentia' and 'Papittedo' in Mildenhall), but they may have held important positions in the late Roman administration, for instance the civil service, or perhaps the army. Perhaps they had been presented with some of these items in recognition of their importance. Or they might simply have been wealthy businessmen or women, like the possible owner of the Cunetio hoard, or wealthy landowning families (see p. 69).

Secondly, they can tell us something about how people were reacting to what were almost certainly difficult or unsettled times. Even though our historical sources are poor, we do know that the Roman administration and army had left the province by about AD 410, a date usually seen as the 'official' end of Roman Britain. Perhaps this created great uncertainty amongst some of those left behind. This was also a time when Britain may have been subject to attacks from continental Europe – the beginnings of the Anglo-Saxon invasions – although finding hard evidence to support this, beyond the accounts from later writers, is once again difficult. So burial of wealth might be linked to these events: either the owners were themselves part of the Roman administration or army, or they were in fear of outside invaders. In either circumstance, they buried their wealth for safekeeping, hoping to return to collect it at a later date. The careful burial of Hoxne, as demonstrated in the discussion of its reconstructed chest, tells us that this was almost certainly the intention.

We shall never know why neither hoard was retrieved. If the owners lived in East Anglia, and we do not even know this for certain, they may have gone abroad or travelled westwards to avoid or escape from troubles in their own part of the country. They might have been killed or died before they were able to pass on information about the whereabouts of their buried wealth. Even if this information were passed on, perhaps relatives failed to work out where their ancestors' precious possessions had been buried – a local landmark used as a reference point, such as a large oak tree, may have long since gone. Whatever the reasons, the loss to the original owners of Mildenhall and Hoxne – and indeed all treasure finds – is very much our gain.

Treasures from medieval and post-medieval Britain

Small but perfectly formed: Anglo-Saxon and medieval treasure

It is generally the case that the further back in time one goes, the less likely it is that material culture will have survived. In the case of objects of metal, finds of the first periods when man began producing objects in both precious and base metals are few and far between, and the range of different artefact types is less diverse than in later periods. Recycling is one reason for this, as metal objects of prehistoric date would often have been melted down and made into new artefacts. Ore sources would also have only been exploited in a relatively limited manner, so the volume of metal objects produced would have been far less than in recent times. And survival in the archaeological record is less likely the older the object is, simply because all metalwork – apart from pure gold – will eventually corrode back into its natural ore state.

By the medieval period, a huge range of different metal objects of gold, silver, lead, tin, copper and iron, alloyed in different combinations, was being manufactured, reaching a peak much later in the mass production centres of the Industrial Revolution. The population of medieval Britain was much larger than that of the Bronze Age to Roman period, and tended to move around much more. These two factors mean that many medieval objects survive in the archaeological record. Some survive

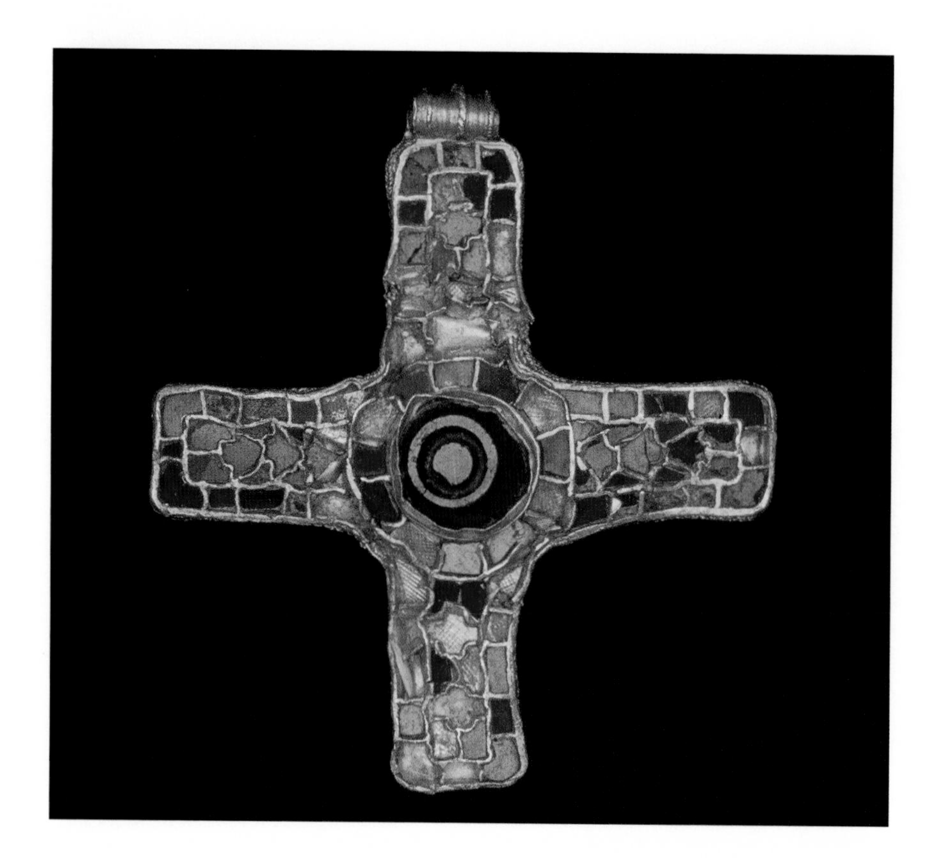

59 The Holderness Cross, East Yorkshire, seventh century AD.

because they were deliberately buried and never recovered – for example, coin hoards dating to the English Civil Wars (see p. 92). But many metal artefacts, from coins to personal trinkets, would have been lost accidentally. Some of the medieval material lost in urban centres is found during excavations – but it can also be found outside in rural places, as rubbish (for instance middens) was often taken out of towns and spread over farmland. This may explain the discovery of the 'BALDEHILDIS' seal ring (see opposite), which was perhaps lost in Norwich but discovered outside when rubbish from inside the city was re-deposited.

When rediscovered, these medieval finds can be of major importance. Often small, very personal items, they can sometimes be linked to historical evidence which may tell us something about who the owners were and how the objects were used. Some examples of these extraordinary objects are provided here.

The Holderness Cross

Date of discovery: c. *1968; date of burial or loss: seventh century AD*

The discovery of the Holderness Cross (fig. 59) is one of the most bizarre accidental discoveries ever made. It was found by a farmer, Ronald Wray, in the late 1960s. Mr Wray was simply walking through one of the fields on his pig farm when his eye caught a glint of gold. He pulled out of the ground a small gold cross, probably brought to the surface by a pig scrabbling around in the soil. After washing the cross to remove the dirt, he dried it and kept it in a drawer in his sideboard, and thought nothing more of it.

It was not until thirty years later that the cross was made public. Mr Wray's daughter saw that a finds identification day was being held at Hull Museum in March 1998, and suggested that she take along the cross for identification. The identification day was being run by Ceinwen Paynton, the Finds Liaison Officer for the region at the time with the Portable Antiquities Scheme (see p. 27). Ceinwen immediately recognised the importance of the piece, and asked if she could take in the find for further study.

What Mr Wray had not realised was that the cross was more than 1,300 years old. It dates to the first half of the seventh century AD, and is a gold cross set with garnets.[16] It has a diameter of only 5 cm. The cross has a suspension loop at the end of one of its arms, which meant it could have been hung from a chain as a pendant. It is undoubtedly a Christian object, and perhaps belonged to someone in the early church.

Because it had been found many years earlier, it was decided at a coroner's inquest that it did not qualify as Treasure, as the Treasure Act cannot be applied retrospectively. Subsequently, the cross was sold at auction and acquired by the Ashmolean Museum in Oxford. Had it not been taken to the finds identification day, it might still be sitting in a sideboard drawer in the finder's kitchen.

THE 'BALDEHILDIS' SEAL RING

Date of discovery: 1998; date when lost or buried: probably late seventh century AD

The 'BALDEHILDIS' seal ring[17] was discovered near Norwich in Norfolk in April 1998 by a local metal detector user (fig. 60). It is a personal seal which can be swivelled so that each side could be used to make a different impression. It would originally have been attached to a finger-ring, the remains of which are still lost and probably unlikely to be found. On one side, the die has a facing bust of a man or woman with simple strands of hair on either side and stylised drapery. On top of the head is a cross, and around the edges is the name 'BALDEHILDIS'. On the other side are two figures facing each other. The one on the right is of a woman who, like the bust on the other side, also has long hair. Facing her on the left is the figure of a bald man with a long wispy beard and large oval eyes. The couple may be engaged in sexual intercourse, as shown in the drawing made from an impression (fig. 61), or the seal may represent a crude attempt at copying a common image on Byzantine betrothal rings.

So who was Baldehildis? By comparison with contemporary Frankish coins, it is believed that the piece dates to the middle of the seventh century AD. So we are therefore looking for a figure, who may have had connections with East Anglia – because of the findspot – who lived around this time. Interestingly, the form of the

60 The 'BALDEHILDIS' seal ring, found near Norwich, Norfolk, dating to the late seventh century AD.

name as written on the seal is Frankish, which would suggest that it originated in France. Even more significant is the fact that there is, in this instance, a historically attested 'Balthildis', whose life is described in the *Vita Sanctae Balthildis*, written in the late seventh century AD. This manuscript describes Balthildis as an English slave[18] who was captured and taken to France, and eventually married Clovis II, the Frankish king, in about AD 648. Upon his death in about AD 657, she acted as Queen-regent which effectively made her ruler of the Frankish kingdom. She died in about 680 at the monastery at Chelles, near Paris, which she founded and retired to in about AD 664 or 665.

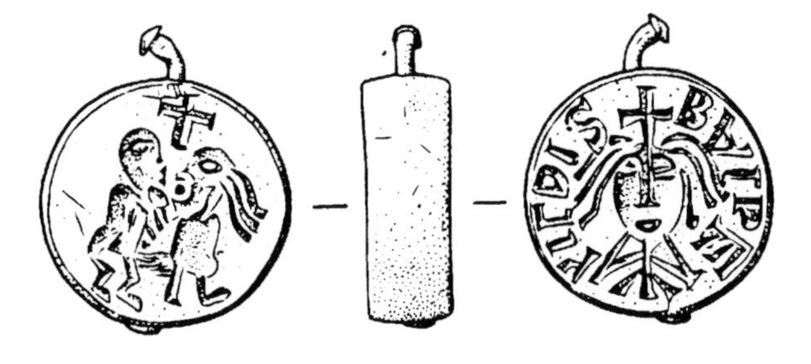

61 A drawing of the 'BALDEHILDIS' seal ring.

To have both a historical account of someone's life and an object with that person's name on is an extremely rare occurrence for treasure. In this case, we will probably never know for certain if the two things can be connected: much more research needs to be conducted. Nevertheless it is already of huge importance, as it is by far the earliest post-Roman seal ring ever to be found in England. And if it really did belong to the historically attested Balthildis, then it would provide an internationally important connection between the East Anglian Royal family and France in the seventh century AD.

The Buntingford figurine

Date of discovery: 1999; date of burial or loss: late thirteenth or early fourteenth century AD

Another religious artefact, like the Thwaite cross described earlier (see p. 21), was discovered near Buntingford in Hertfordshire in 1999 (fig. 62). Less than 5 cm in height, the object is a silver-gilt figure of a saint or Old Testament character such as a prophet.[19] The figure is a bearded man, with a calm and rather serious face, and downcast eyes. He is wearing a hooded and belted tunic which comes down to his feet. His left arm and hand are unfortunately missing, but his right arm is still intact. His right fist is clenched as if it is holding some object – if there were previously something there this has now broken away, which is unfortunate as it might have provided a clue to his identity.

The figure almost certainly belonged to a shrine, casket or a piece of statuary, and would have been attached by the feet. There is also a loop

62 A silver-gilt figurine from the Buntingford area, Hertfordshire, late thirteenth to early fourteenth century AD. The white line shows its actual size.

on the back of the figure which would have helped to secure it. At some point, therefore, the figure became detached from this object, perhaps deliberately, and later became accidentally lost. We do not know its original location, but, like the Thwaite cross, it probably resided in an ecclesiastical establishment such as a local church, rather than a private home.

The Chiddingly boar

Date of discovery: 1999; date of loss or burial: late fifteenth century AD

63 The Chiddingly boar cap-badge, East Sussex, late fifteenth century AD. The black line shows its actual size.

Another metal detector discovery made in 1999 was a badge in the form of a boar (fig. 63) found at Chiddingly, East Sussex. The object is tiny, measuring just over 3 cm across, is made of silver, and would have originally been gilded. On the back are the remains of a setting for a pin, and it seems highly likely that it was intended to be worn on a hat.

In a similar manner to the 'BALDEHILDIS' seal ring described above, there is a strong link which can be made between this object and the historical sources. The badge dates to the late fifteenth century AD, the reign of King Richard III (1483–5). It is well known that between about 1470 and 1485, the boar was used by the household and followers of Richard III as a symbol of allegiance. Records of the Royal Wardrobe accounts of 1483 tell us that thousands of boar badges were produced for use at occasions such as Richard III's coronation in July of that year.[20] But this is the first instance where an example made of a precious metal has been discovered – most cap-badges of this type were made of base metals such as pewter.

Sword and scabbard fittings

Another important class of medieval object is fittings for swords and scabbards. One particularly attractive example is a fitting found with a metal detector near Bury St Edmunds, Suffolk, in 2000, by Lady Kemball (fig. 64, left).[21] It is a gold pyramidal mount dating to the first half of the seventh century AD, decorated with an inset garnet at the top, and with delicate filigree (wire) ornament on each of its four sides in the form of a series of snake-like intertwined knots.

This pyramidal fitting would have been attached to a strap which held a sword and its scabbard to a sword-belt. About one hundred of these fittings are known, but few are made of gold. Most examples found in Britain are stray finds. Examples as well made as this would originally have belonged to an important Anglo-Saxon individual.

65 The Tregwynt English Civil War coin hoard, Pembrokeshire, buried around AD 1648. The hoard is the largest of its type discovered in Wales to date.

The 'BALDEHILDIS' seal ring, Buntingford figurine and Chiddingly boar badge are just three examples of small medieval objects which, as individual items, have added to our understanding of the medieval period in Britain. All were probably accidental losses, unlike the coin and silver plate hoards which were buried deliberately as a reaction to troubled times during the English Civil Wars.

Times of crisis: coin hoards of the English Civil Wars

Dates of discovery: various (Tregwynt, 1996); dates of burial: AD 1642–51

There are a number of references in literature to the burial of treasure, the most famous of these perhaps being the account given by Samuel Pepys in June 1667 of him sending his wife and father from London to conceal £1,300 at his country estate at Brampton, Northamptonshire (see p. 40). In this case, we have an account of the burial of personal possessions, but not the actual objects themselves, for Pepys was able to go back and retrieve them. In the vast majority of cases where treasure is discovered, no such account exists.

There is one episode, however, in the history of the British Isles when well-attested historical events can be linked directly to the burial of treasures which have been rediscovered in modern times.[22] To date, there have been over 200 discoveries of coin hoards which can be dated to the time of the English Civil Wars (1642–51). This episode in British history was a bitter and bloody struggle which affected all levels of society. On one side stood the Parliamentarians, also known as the Roundheads, who stood for the privileges and rights of Parliament. The most well known of the Parliamentarians was Oliver Cromwell. On the other side stood King Charles I and his supporters, the Royalists or Cavaliers, who believed that power should rest with the monarch.

The war also dragged on in Scotland, Ireland and Wales. The largest Welsh coin hoard of this time was discovered at Tregwynt Mansion near Fishguard in Pembrokeshire in 1996 (fig. 65).[23] The find came to light during construction work for a new tennis court which involved a local metal detectorist, Roy Lewis, who was asked to scan the spoil. It was fortunate that Roy did this, as he soon discovered fifty-five silver coins of the sixteenth and seventeenth centuries. After further digging, detecting uncovered a total of 33 gold and 467 silver coins, alongside a sheet of lead, some pottery fragments and a gold finger-ring.

The Tregwynt hoard is one of the finest coin hoards ever found on Welsh soil. At the time of deposit it was worth £51 and 9 shillings which would have paid fifty foot soldiers for a month or bought about 2 tons of cheese.[24] In real terms today this would be a sizeable sum, somewhere in the region of £5,000 to £10,000. For people who study coins, the hoard is extremely important, as it contains a large number of interesting and rare issues from a time of major upheaval. These include coins from temporary mints established by King Charles I to fund the costs of the war, the first of which was set up at Shrewsbury in September 1642. An example is a half crown with a clear propaganda – if somewhat ironic – message referring to the king's specific war aims: to maintain the Protestant religion, the laws of England, and the liberty of Parliament ('RELIG. PROT. LEG ANG. LIBERT. PAR'). The date, unusual on coins of the time, is also prominent, and it is possible that this coin was used to pay a foot soldier before the first major battle, at Edgehill on 23 October 1642.

66 A bust of Oliver Cromwell, the most well known of the Parliamentarians during the English Civil Wars. This terracotta sculpture is by Louis-François Roubiliac, and was made in London around AD 1759.

Who owned the Tregwynt hoard and why was it buried and never recovered? The last part of this question is perhaps easier to answer than the first. The latest coin in the hoard dates to either 1647 or 1648, so the whole assemblage is likely to have been buried very soon after that. The most obvious event of that date which could account for the burial and non-retrieval of the hoard is the so-called 'Second Civil War', a series of Royalist uprisings in the spring of 1648. One of these uprisings was in Pembrokeshire where the treasure was buried. Events were serious enough for Oliver Cromwell himself to come to west Wales to besiege Pembroke Castle, which did not surrender until 11 July 1648 (fig. 66). The involvement of the owner of the hoard in these events seems highly likely.

As for the actual owner, inconclusive evidence comes from the site of burial itself and from one of the items in the hoard. The treasure was hidden in an outbuilding on the estate at Tregwynt, which at the time was in the ownership of Llewellin Harries, who had at least six sons and six daughters – so maybe he or one of his offspring was responsible for the burial. If so, he clearly had not relayed this information to any of his family, or if he did, they were for some reason unable to retrieve the treasure. The most personal item in the assemblage is a gold 'posy' or motto ring (also discussed on p. 131) with the legend 'Rather death then falce of fayth' ('Rather death than false of faith'), but unfortunately this does not provide any further clues as to the owner. The message is rather ambiguous, as it could relate to a personal relationship such as marriage, or alternatively to political or religious adherence. Regardless of who buried the hoard, knowledge of its location was soon lost.

There are many possible explanations as to why hoards of the Civil War were hidden, or rather why they were never recovered. Some people might have prudently hidden a cache of money at an early stage in the war, but died before they felt comfortable with the idea of recovering it. This may account for the biggest single group of hoards – nearly forty – which date to the start of the armed conflict (*c.* 1642–3). People with strong sympathies may have left money hidden while they went to join the rival armies, or just moved into a safer part of the country, still hoping to return fairly soon. As the war continued, money might have been buried to hide it from raiders, local garrisons, or from the levies ordained by local Parliamentary or Royalist officials. Towards the end of the war, Royalist supporters suffered sequestrations (when possessions were taken away in lieu of a monetary payment) which they would have wanted to minimise. This might explain the burial of the Armada service (see box opposite).

Although hoards are known from almost every part of the country, the course of the struggle was clearly an important factor in where they were actually buried. Many people were affected by specific campaigns of the war, and concentrations of hoards in different areas may reflect this. Thus, groups of hoards can be associated with great sieges, such as those on the towns of Gloucester and Newark. Many hoards come from the areas which saw the most fighting, particularly in the borderlands between regions which were either strongly Royalist or Parliamentarian, such as Oxfordshire where the king had his head-quarters, and parts of the West Midlands, south and west Yorkshire. Areas associated with the risings of the 'Second Civil War' have produced significant coin hoards such as Tregwynt. The crucial fact is probably that no one foresaw that the struggle would take so long or be so disruptive, or that so many people would face death, displacement, dispossession or long exile, all of which prevented the recovery of a great deal of treasure.

The finding of Civil War hoards can thus be connected with the disruption to families and communities which resulted from this difficult period. We should remember, however, that these are only a sample. Many other hoards were no doubt recovered by their owners once the opportunity arose, and their contents were put back into circulation. Some were perhaps re-hoarded in the later seventeenth century, to be found again in modern times. All the silver coinage of the Civil War years was finally swept from circulation in the Great Recoinage of 1696–8.

Not the end of the story

This chapter has looked at a number of treasure finds, the stories behind their discovery and, most importantly, what they can tell us about the periods in our history to which they belong. The next chapter looks at a different type of object: small, forgotten pieces from the past, not necessarily made of gold or silver which, taken as groups, have an equally important story to tell.

The Armada service

In addition to coin hoards, there are other sets of precious objects which were almost certainly buried deliberately during the English Civil Wars. The best example is the so-called 'Armada service', a set of twenty-six silver-gilt vessels discovered in a potato barn near Radford in Devon in 1827 (fig. 67).[25] There is good evidence to suggest that it was concealed some time between 1645 and 1648, in the latter stages of the war. Engravings on the pieces of the heraldic arms of Sir Christopher Harris of Radford and his wife, Mary Sydenham, provide us with a rare instance of knowing who the actual owners were (these crests also meant that, when discovered, the find was not declared as Treasure Trove as the descendants of Christopher Harris were able to lay claim to it). Knowing to whom the service belonged meant that it could be tied in with events surrounding the Harris family and their Devonshire estates. Harris was a known Royalist, and would have come under the gaze of the Parliamentarians who gained major ground in the region in 1645. Local Royalists, including Harris, had their property assessed for worth, and in some cases it was taken away. Thus the silver may well have been hidden at this time in order to reduce the value of his holdings. Alternatively, the silver may have been buried at the time of his death in order to prevent it from being melted down to pay off a debt which we know existed from Harris's will. Whatever the circumstances, this particular find demonstrates very well that, when combined with historical sources, some treasures can tell us interesting stories about our past and the ways people sought to protect their most prized possessions.

67 The 'Armada service', a set of twenty-six silver-gilt vessels dated to AD 1581–1601.

4

Small Things Forgotten

Introduction

> 'It is terribly important that the "small things forgotten" be remembered. For in the seemingly little and insignificant things that accumulate to create a lifetime, the essence of our existence is captured. We must remember these bits and pieces, and we must use them in new and imaginative ways so that a different appreciation of what life is today, and was in the past, can be achieved. The written document has its proper and important place but there is also a time when we should set aside our perusal of diaries, court records, and inventories, and listen to another voice.
>
> Don't read what we have written; look at what we have done.'[1]

Major treasure finds have their own stories to tell about life in the past (see Chapter 3). These treasures are characteristically large, shiny, often priceless pieces that almost demand us to listen to what they are saying about our past. But such treasures are rare. The vast majority of archaeological finds are small, unglamorous, sometimes broken, and usually financially worthless. Despite this, they too have a story to tell, and it is important that we do not underestimate their place in the fabric of our heritage. Arguably these small objects of everyday life are more important pieces of the past as their story is about ordinary peoples' lives on a day-to-day basis, not about the world of the rich and exceptional as told through the discovery of major treasures.

For all periods of British history, people have used a huge range of objects made from a variety of materials, from organic substances such as bone, to minerals such as metal and stone. These objects were sometimes accidentally lost, deliberately discarded or deliberately buried, and the discovery of these in modern times has led to major changes in the way we look at the lives of people in the past. Our knowledge of the objects has been transformed since the advent of the metal detector which has provided specialists with many new discoveries of both individual finds and new archaeological sites.

Some of the work which is being conducted on these 'small things forgotten' is discussed in this chapter. Extraordinary discoveries of ancient stone artefacts have transformed our picture of earliest history, and are even more remarkable as the objects discussed were found entirely by amateurs (see pp. 99–102). This chapter also looks at objects worn by people at different times in the past, either as jewellery or as dress accessories. These include one of the most constantly worn small items of all historical periods from Roman times to the present day – the finger-ring (see pp. 127–33); gold objects worn by people during the Bronze Age, the exact function of which, in some cases, we are still struggling to understand (see pp. 102–7); and one of the major classes of object about which we have learnt so much since the 1996 Treasure Act – dress-fittings fashionable during Tudor times (see pp. 123–7). This chapter also discusses other classes of find which have the potential to change our view of different periods in our past completely, and which have largely come to us through the discoveries of amateur finders. These include objects used for personal hygiene and cosmetics from Iron Age and Roman Britain (see pp. 107–10); finds of metalwork which tell us about the daily lives of people during the Viking period in different parts of England and Wales (see pp. 110–18); and miniature objects from the Middle Ages, which tell us that toys had a more important role in medieval and later society than was previously thought (see pp. 118–23).

Finding the first Britons

Date range: c. *700,000–4,000* BC

Throughout this book, the role of the metal detectorist in discovering pieces of our history has been a recurring theme. But people in the past did not only make and use things made of metal – in fact, metal objects have only been around in this country for just over 4,000 years. Other amateur archaeologists and ordinary members of the public, relying purely on their own eyes, have made discoveries from much earlier times which show that people have been shaping the environment of Britain for at least 500,000 years. Their finds are made of stone, one of the first substances used by mankind to fashion artefacts.

Almost all that survives from this ancient period are triangular shaped stone tools called hand-axes. These were made by human-like people who lived in Britain at different times during the Ice Ages – periods when much of Britain was covered by glaciers and ice – which occurred between 500,000 and 40,000 years ago. These people lived in small groups which often travelled long distances to hunt animals and gather plants for food. For the last 200 years, many thousands of these hand-axes have been discovered in southern Britain, and a number have found their way to museums. They have usually been unearthed not by professional archaeologists, but by interested amateurs or workers in gravel and sand quarries. These sands and gravels are often the deposits left at the bottom of ancient rivers which date to the Ice Ages.

Until recently, archaeologists thought that 'stray' hand-axes picked up by amateurs, as opposed to those recovered during the course of professional archaeological investigations, could not tell us much about our distant past. However, recent research has accurately plotted where many of these amateur discoveries have been made over the last 200 years. This research has led to a number of interesting insights into these objects, for example clear patterns in common types of hand-axe in different parts of Britain. But this only came about because amateur finders reported and donated their finds to local museums, and most importantly have at times provided accurate information as to where they made their discoveries. Two of these individual finders are discussed here: Mike Chambers and Phil Shepherd.

The earliest stone axe?

Mike Chambers began beachcombing on the shoreline of north-east Norfolk in the early 1990s. Finding anything from fossils to parts of Second World War aircraft, Mike made his most significant discovery in February 2000, when he stumbled across a flint hand-axe (fig. 68).[2] Mike reported his discovery to Norfolk Museums Service, where the axe is now kept, and was highly commended for his discovery in the Tarmac Finder's Award at the British Archaeological Awards held in Liverpool in 2002.

To the untrained eye, Mike's discovery might not seem particularly exciting. It is a flint which, like thousands of other flint tools, had been deliberately worked into a triangular point. This would allow it to have been used as a blade, for example to joint an animal. It is not the function or form of Mike's axe which makes it so unusual, however, but its age. This hand-axe is probably the oldest humanly made object ever found in Britain or, indeed, north-west Europe.

At present, it is unclear exactly how old the hand-axe is, but it is undoubtedly extremely ancient. Some specialists have dated it to 700,000 BC, but more cautious estimates have placed it at around 550,000 years old. More research is now taking place at the site where the axe was discovered in order to date it more accurately. Crucial to this work will be establishing exactly where the axe came from in the nearby cliff-face from which it had been eroded. Unlike much later historical periods, when methods such as radiocarbon dating can be used to age material, archaeologists studying this find will need to be clear about the geological strata from which the axe emerged. Whatever this work eventually reveals about the dating of this axe, it is the link with our earliest ancestors that is the most important aspect of this discovery. It may show us that early man was living in Britain far longer than was previously thought – even earlier, perhaps, than material from Boxgrove, West Sussex, and Westbury, Somerset. Thus the discovery of one enthusiastic – and most importantly, responsible – amateur finder has the potential to revolutionise understanding of our ancient origins.

Secrets of the Welsh forests

Not all stone tools that are found are as ancient as Mike Chambers' discovery – most are between 10,000 and 4,000 years old. Finds from this period are nonetheless also important clues to the past, especially if it is known exactly where they were found. Most stone tools from this date are stray finds, picked up by people out walking or going about their work. One such finder is Phil Shepherd, who started noticing flint tools during the course of his work for the Forestry Commission in south Wales (fig. 70).[3] For over twenty-five years he has systematically collected these, noting exactly where he found them, and donating them to the National Museums & Galleries of Wales in Cardiff. Details are also lodged with the Forestry Commission itself and the Glamorgan-Gwent Archaeological Trust.

Phil Shepherd's discoveries have included a Neolithic flint sickle and a hoard of Early Bronze Age flint scrapers (figs 69, 71). But even more important are the hundreds of tiny flint tools he has collected called 'microliths'. These small objects, less than ½ cm long, are the type of tools typical of the period, 10,000 to 5,000 years ago, which is often referred to as the Mesolithic or Middle Stone Age (fig. 72). When Mr Shepherd's discoveries are plotted on a map, it is possible to build up a picture of where people lived in south Wales, and the areas in which they hunted. Microliths were used as arrowheads for hunting game. The pieces of waste flint produced from

68 Mike Chambers' palaeolithic hand-axe: the earliest known humanly made artefact ever found in Britain? The axe is thought to be at least 550,000 years old.

69 A hoard of flint scrapers of the early Bronze Age recovered by Phil Shepherd.

70 Phil Shepherd at the National Museums & Galleries of Wales.

71 A flint sickle recovered by Phil Shepherd in south Wales.

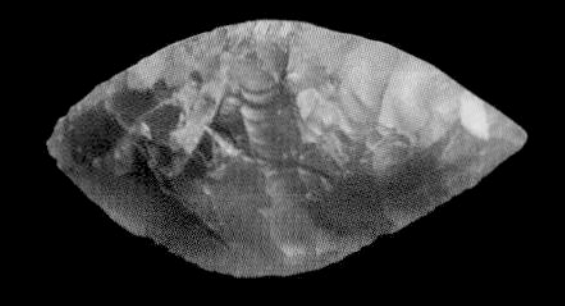

72 A Mesolithic flint arrowhead, one of a large number of 'microliths' recovered by Phil Shepherd.

making these objects show where people actually sat and worked on them, and the microliths themselves indicate where hunted animals were struck by them when fired from a bow, and the instances when arrows went astray.

Very few flint tools had been found in this part of Wales before Mr Shepherd started his hobby, which means that he has made a significant contribution to understanding Welsh prehistory. Like Mike Chambers, Phil's work was also recognised by the British Archaeological Awards, when he won the Tarmac Finder's Award in 2000.

73 A range of penannular gold rings dating to the late Bronze Age, one of the most unusual types of treasure find. Their exact function remains unclear, but they were almost certainly used for body adornment. The largest ring (top left) is 38 mm in diameter.

Body adornment in the Bronze Age

Date range: c. *1150–750* BC

Among the most perplexing objects found regularly by metal detectorists in Britain are small thick penannular rings (fig. 73). These have a narrow central hole, unlike finger-rings discussed at the end of this chapter, and a gap in the ring itself (which is the meaning of the term penannular). They are made of gold which may contain variable amounts of silver, and can be plain or striped in appearance. Sometimes they have a copper or lead core covered with a gold wrapping. They have been found in many parts of Britain, but never in association with other archaeological remains – for instance, burials – which means that few have an archaeological context. These rings date to the late Bronze Age (*c.* 1150–750 BC).

What were these curious objects used for? They were originally referred to by early antiquarians as 'ring money' because they were thought to have been used as primitive currency, and this description is still sometimes used, incorrectly, today. One of the reasons for the survival of this idea probably stems from the fact that some gold ornaments, particularly a type of bracelet with expanded terminals known from the Irish Bronze Age, bear a remarkable resemblance to a kind of currency called the manilla. Manillas were used in West Africa, for example on the Gold Coast and Sierre Leone, from as long ago as the fifteenth century AD until 1948.[4] They have come to be associated with the slave trade, and were used both as a form of local currency and as ornaments. But, apart from the general shape of these objects, there are few other similarities. The West African manillas were made of copper or brass, not precious metal, and are of a much later date. So the idea that we should see the Bronze Age rings as currency has little to support it. In any case, Bronze Age penannular rings do not have one of the key requirements of currency, as they are not of fixed weight or material. The earliest recognisable coinages produced in Britain date to at least 500 years later, to about the second century BC, and there is no reason to think that money was in use so much earlier in our history.

So if not a form of currency, what were they used for? It is almost certain that they were a form of personal adornment. There are two ways in which they might have been worn, but one does not necessarily preclude the other. The first theory is that they were worn in the hair, as tress-rings (an earlier type of possible tress-ring is known from the grave of the Amesbury archer; see p. 53). In such circumstances, the hair would have been braided and the ring forced over the braids by pushing the hair into the gap.

The problem with the tress-ring idea is that the function of the break in the ring is not entirely clear. Such a break would not have been necessary for these rings to function as hair adornments – hair could have been pushed through the central hole in the ring without the need for a break. But the break was clearly very important, as all the rings are made like this. The other alternative, therefore, is that the rings were worn not in the hair, but somewhere on the body, most likely the face or head. The most attractive proposition to date is that they were worn as nose-rings, with the gap pushed over the septum of the nose (this may well have been quite painful as the gaps tend to be narrow, but it was perhaps done at a young age when the nose was much smaller). This idea is also attractive for two other reasons. Firstly, the rings bear similarities with pre-Columbian nose-rings from central and southern America.[5] Secondly, close examination of the rings has shown that they often have wear on the outer surface, which implies that this was the area where they were handled most. If they were being taken on and off the nose, this might explain the wear pattern, although, of course, there are other parts of the face where they could have been worn, for instance lips, ears, or even eyebrows, and other parts of the body such as the nipple. However, these seem less likely than the nose because it is not clear how they would have stayed on. If the gap in the rings had a pin, then this would have been able to pierce the skin – for instance of an earlobe – more effectively; but none has been discovered with a suitable pin. So the nose seems, at present, the most likely option.

These rings are not the only type of body ornament known from this period. Recent work in Ireland has shown that another mystery gold object was probably also worn to decorate the head (fig. 74).[6] These particular objects, which look similar to bobbins used on sewing machines, comprise two circular discs of sheet gold with a central recess in-between. The theory is that they were ear-spools, worn inside a grossly distended earlobe. There are strong ethnographic parallels for these ear-spools, particularly in Africa, where weights are used to extend a hole in the earlobe, allowing an ear-spool to be worn when the hole was large enough. Ear-spools are also known from other ancient cultures, such as Egypt, and are worn by some in modern-day Western society. Both ear-spools and piercings of every conceivable part

74 An artist's impression of how some items used for body adornment might have been worn during the Bronze Age. These include ear-spools and a sheet metal *lunula* necklace.

of the head and body have become increasingly popular amongst the young in the last few decades, influenced by the Punk movement of the 1970s and the popularity of ethnic fashions originating in Africa and Asia.

Ear-spools support the idea that penannular rings, as another unusual class of jewellery, could have been worn in a way which is not immediately obvious to the modern eye. In any case, these penannular rings are in good company, as there are other forms of gold jewellery for which we have a clearer idea of the function. These include early Bronze Age *lunulae* (fig. 75), which are sheet gold necklaces not dissimilar to those shown in figure 74; bracelets, sometimes with expanded terminals, and armlets, probably worn on the upper arm, which date to the middle to late Bronze Age.

All these jewellery items were a way of indicating one's position in Bronze Age society. Gold and particularly silver were not readily available at this period in mainland Britain, and those who were able to acquire precious metal must have been important individuals. In addition, the quality of the work on many of these jewellery items is extremely high. Close scientific examination of the penannular rings shows that some were very carefully constructed: the striped ones, in particular, had much time and skill invested in them (figs 76–7). On these, a silver-rich gold wire, whitish in colour, was wound around a rod of yellow gold, which had been spirally grooved to take the inlay. This was then heated and burnished or gently hammered to fuse the silvery wire to the gold, and then bent into the ring shape.[7] These striped rings must have been

75 A gold *lunula* necklace from Blessington, County Wicklow, Ireland, dated to the early Bronze Age.

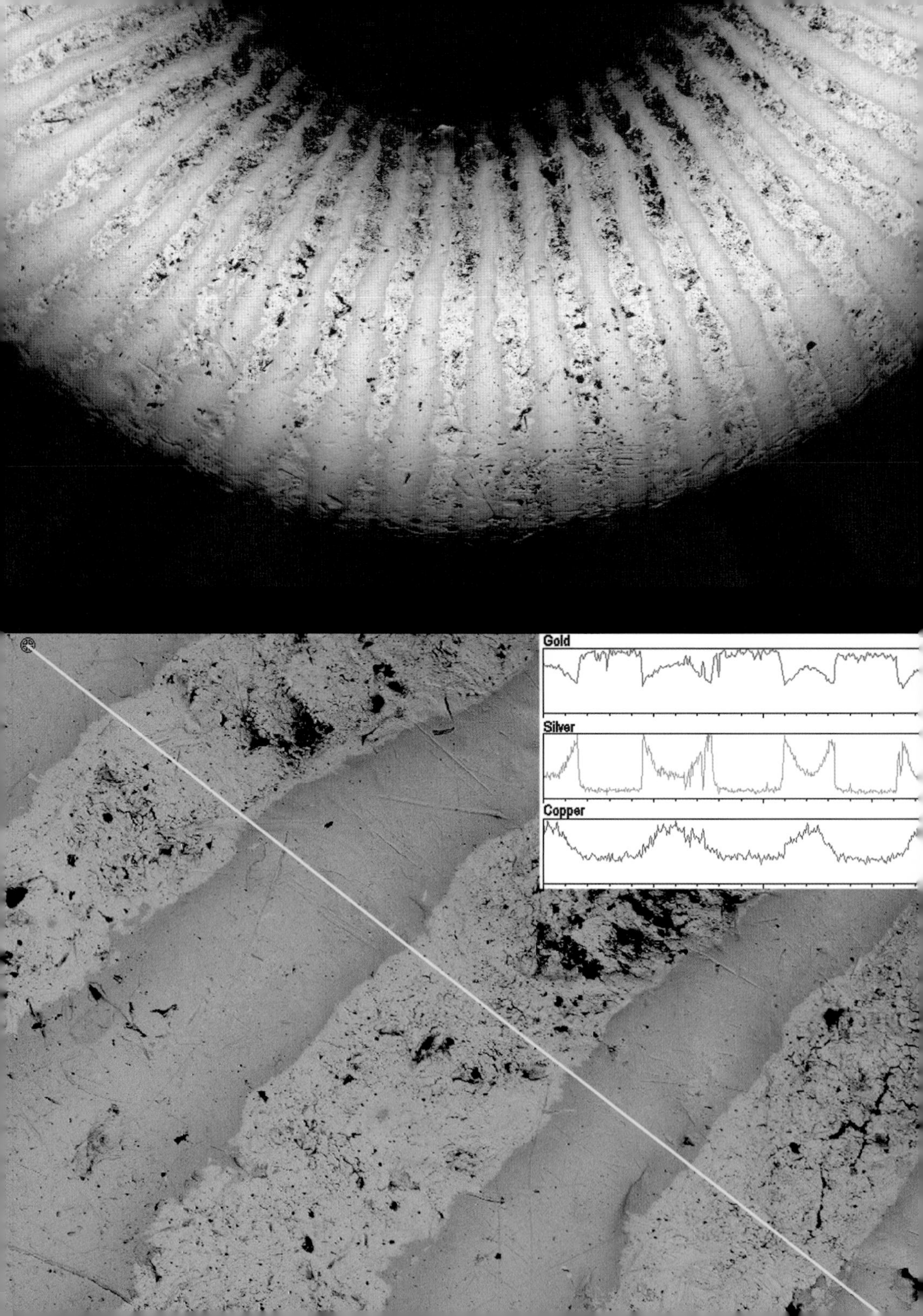
Gold
Silver
Copper

76 A penannular gold ring (fig. 73, below right of large ring) under high magnification in a Scanning Electron Microscope (SEM). A special imaging detector was used to emphasise the compositional differences between the gold and silvery stripes. Note how the stripes taper towards the inside of the ring, showing how the ring was made of a straight gold rod that was spiral wound with the silvery wire and then bent into shape.

77 Microscopic (SEM) image of the penannular ring (fig. 76). The darker stripes are the silvery plated wire. Superimposed is an x-ray line scan (yellow line) for the concentrations of gold, silver and copper (coloured graphs). The red graph shows how the concentrations of silver varies across the stripes. This shows that the goldsmith silver-plated a gold wire before inlaying it into the gold ring – a sophisticated technique to make the silver, very scarce in the Bronze Age, go further.

more valued than the plain ones, and when worn would probably have marked out these people as being exceptional individuals in a community.

Thus a Bronze Age mystery object may be in the process of being solved. These curious rings should be considered as part of a range of jewellery worn by ancient Britons to show off their wealth or help them to stand out as important members of society. This should come as no particular surprise, as other items of Bronze Age gold, such as the Mold cape, were almost certainly used to define status (see p. 42). By the Iron Age (*c.* 700 BC–AD 50/100), however, these gold rings seem to have fallen out of use. It is not until the late Iron Age, around the second century BC, that a completely new form of jewellery – the torc, or neck-ring – was introduced (see pp. 60 and 137). At the end of this period, these too had fallen out of favour, and there is evidence that different methods were being used by people to distinguish themselves from others: not only jewellery, but grooming and cosmetics, a subject to which we can now turn.

Keeping up appearances in Iron Age and Roman Britain

Date range: first century BC to fourth century AD

The use of objects to adorn the body is discussed in a number of places in this book. In Bronze Age Britain, some people probably wore ornate necklaces and rings, possibly worn on the nose or in the hair, to denote their social status (see above). Finger-rings have been used for centuries in a similar manner (see p. 127), as have dress-fittings in Tudor times (see p. 123). But there have always been other means by which people could modify their appearance, aside from wearing jewellery. Clothing and different hairstyles are two obvious examples, but these rarely leave direct traces in the archaeological record. But two other practices sometimes do: wearing cosmetics and grooming, for example plucking eyebrows. One of the earliest periods for which we have evidence of these activities in Britain is around 2,000 years ago, from the end of the Iron Age and the Roman period.[8]

Evidence that people were grooming themselves or wearing cosmetics comes from a range of objects. These appear in the archaeological record during the first century BC, and continued to be used, it seems, for about another three to four hundred years, probably into the fourth century AD. Archaeologists have excavated these objects from a number of different sites, from settlements to cremation graves; and in the last few decades, the number of these objects known has grown dramatically through metal detector discoveries. Most have been found in southern parts of Britain.

The objects fall into two groups. The first category of find is a set of objects used to clean the body, particularly the face and hands, which archaeologists often call 'toilet implements' or 'toilet sets'. The first of the set is a nail cleaner for fingers and toes – a two-pronged slender bronze implement, a few centimetres long. The second is a pair of tweezers, probably used for many of the same purposes as today, such as the removal of splinters and loose bits of skin from hands, and for plucking hairs from all parts of the face and head.[9] Both nail cleaners and tweezers can be plain, simple, and even quite crudely made, but were sometimes finely decorated. They are both very recognisable types of object still in use today – there is little difference in shape between a pair of tweezers bought in a high-street chemist and one recovered from a Roman settlement of 2,000 years ago. The third item often found in these 'toilet sets', for which there is not such an obvious modern parallel (at least in terms of grooming implements), is a small scoop. Though smaller, these are not dissimilar in appearance to small spoons which accompany salt cellars. They could have been used to clean ears.

All these items are usually found individually, but occasionally they are discovered in sets on a suspension hoop. The hoop would have been attached to a belt or garment to allow the owner to have the set on him or her as they moved around. Alternatively, they were suspended from châtelaine brooches, a type of Roman brooch, usually of the second century AD, which could be pinned to a garment (fig. 78).

Other types of implement, sometimes found with 'toilet sets', are rather more unusual and would not be so easily recognised now. Probes, shaped a little like cotton buds, are sometimes found or form the other end of a small scoop. Their function is less clear, but like scoops were probably used to remove grime from various parts of the body. Surgeons, however, often had similar types of object, and would have used them for a range of purposes, for example to explore wounds. Scoops could also have been used to extract substances from small containers, for example perfumes from small glass phials. Thus, when discovered, it is not always certain that scoops or probes were used purely for body hygiene.[10]

In addition to implements used for cleaning, another distinctive type of bronze object has been found dating to this time, known as a 'cosmetic grinder' (fig. 79). It consists of a mortar, usually shaped like a crescent, with a shallow or deep groove inside. It combines with a rod-like pestle, also usually curved, which fits neatly into the groove. Both are only a few centimetres long, and both almost invariably have a suspension loop, which means that they too could be strung together and perhaps hung from a belt. To date, over 600 examples have been found in Britain,[11] largely as the result of metal detector discoveries. Most date to the second to third centuries AD, are a purely British type, and originated before the Roman invasion of Britain in AD 43.

78 A châtelaine brooch set of toilet implements, including a pair of tweezers, a double-pronged nail cleaner and an 'ear scoop'. This example dates to the second century AD.

Ralph Jackson at the British Museum has conducted the principal research on these curious objects, and his work has been essential for understanding what they were used for. Wear marks on the inside of the grooved mortars, and in some cases on the pestle as well, demonstrate that they were used to grind up a substance, probably pellets or coarse granules, into a fine powder. Although it is not known exactly what this powder would have been used for, coloured cosmetics seem the most likely. These were probably applied to the face like modern make-up, but could have also been used to decorate other parts of the body. An important find from Cheapside, London, in 1955,[12] shows that they were used in combination with a toilet set, as one was found corroded together with a nail cleaner and tweezers. This and other similar finds support the argument that they were used for cosmetics – as is the case today, grooming and cosmetics seemed to go hand in hand.

79 A cosmetic mortar from Hockwold, Norfolk, probably first century AD. This decorated example has the head of a bull at one end and a swan or duck at the other. The suspension loop would have allowed it to be hung from a belt. The pestle part of the set is missing.

Experiments with replica cosmetic sets have shown that the pestle or fingers could have been used to apply the powder (fig. 80). Experiments have also been conducted using a range of possible minerals which might have been used to make colours (see box p. 110). Some of these substances could have been easily obtainable locally, whilst others may have come from different parts of the Roman Empire through trade and other contacts. It should be stressed that at present this is still only a theory – traces of powders have not been found in the mortars, nor have the minerals been found with the cosmetic sets. Nevertheless, showing that it was possible to make these powders is important because it proves that in practice they would have worked very effectively – small amounts of coloured powders could quite easily have been made from these cosmetic grinders.

It should also be made clear that these 'cosmetic grinders' were not used to process woad. Woad was a plant cultivated for its leaves because they produced a blue dye. Caesar tells us that the ancient Britons used woad to paint their bodies blue before going into battle.[13] Cosmetic grinders may indicate that grooming had changed – vegetable dyes, like woad, being superseded by more subtle mineral colours used in smaller quantities.

Toilet sets and cosmetic grinders are extremely interesting objects which raise a number of important questions. Why did they suddenly appear at this time? Toilet items, and particularly cosmetic grinders, are not known from Britain before the first century BC, although items such as nail cleaners are

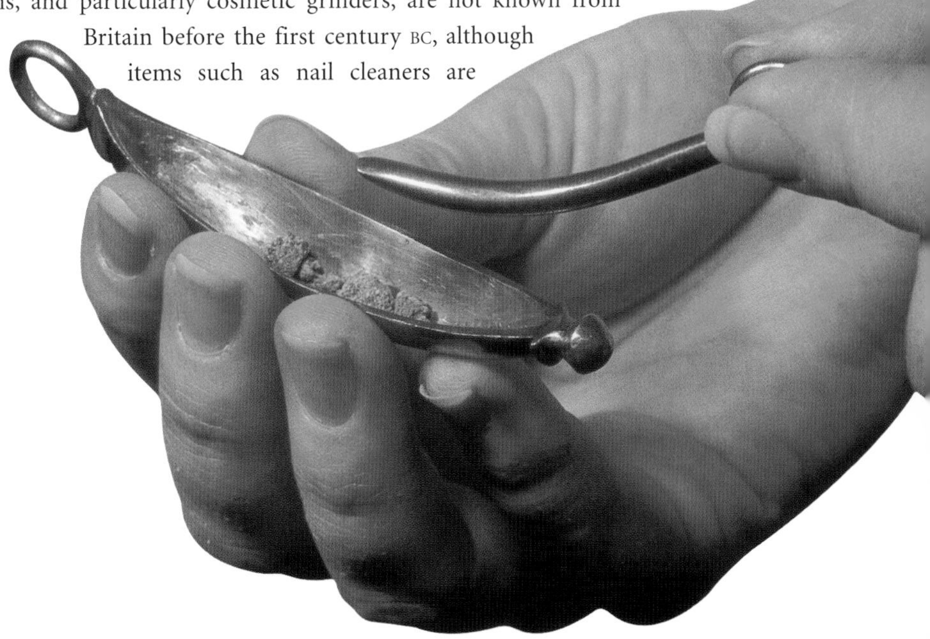

80 A 'cosmetic grinder' replica set in use. Experiments have shown that the pestle and mortar would have been very effective for grinding minerals into powder to use as make-up.

sometimes found on the continent. And some, particularly cosmetic grinders, are *only* found in Britain.[14] Does this mean that people were not interested in grooming or wearing cosmetics before this date? Not necessarily – perhaps they were simply using other implements which have not survived, for instance objects made in wood. And razors, dating to the Bronze Age, at least show that people were trimming their hair. But let us assume that this was to some extent a new fashion – what does that say about people living in Britain at this time? We do not know who owned cosmetic or toilet sets, but those who did obviously felt keen to groom themselves or colour their faces. The fact that sets were often attractively decorated and could be worn on a belt or brooch also shows that the owners were keen to display them for all to see. At all stages in history, certain groups have used these techniques to stand out from the crowd. Punks are an obvious – if somewhat extreme – modern example, as they use hair dyes, make-up, jewellery and clothes to distinguish themselves from others.

We also do not know if these objects were used by men, women, or both (or indeed children), but we should certainly not assume that make-up was only worn by women, as it (mainly) is today. A Roman poet Propertius, writing in the 20s BC, gives a hint that the ancient Britons were known to wear cosmetics, but does not specify who wore them.[15] And we also do not know if it was one particular social group who used these objects, or if their use related to the region in which people lived. Interestingly, nail cleaners seem to show distinct regional patterns,[16] and this fits in with other types of object which are only found in certain parts of the country such as 'dragonesque' brooches, for example.[17] So there is some evidence that implies that people in different parts of Britain were trying to define themselves by using distinctive dress accessories, cosmetics or by different ways of grooming.

Possible substances used for grinding in cosmetic mortars

GALENA (lead sulphide) – silvery grey
AZURITE (a copper carbonate) – blue
MALACHITE (a copper carbonate) – green
GRAPHITE (a form of carbon) – glittery black
ILMENITE (an oxide of iron and titanium) – grey
HAEMATITE (an iron oxide) – red

Thus late Iron Age and Roman toilet and cosmetic implements are particular types of 'small things forgotten' which have an important story to tell about how some people in late Iron Age and early Roman Britain chose to modify their appearance. It is our job to 'read' this story, and try to understand its meaning.

Finding the Vikings

Date range: eighth to eleventh centuries AD

So far this chapter has looked at some specific types of small objects, from flint tools to Bronze Age gold rings, and items used to groom and decorate the body. All these have modified our view of ancient Britain, either helping with the 'when' questions, for example changing our view of when the island was first occupied; or with the 'how' questions, for instance how people used objects to modify their appearance. The vital part played by amateur finders is a common thread throughout. All these finds come from periods when there are either no surviving written accounts or when such evidence is minimal. This makes the study and interpretation of the archaeological evidence all the more essential.

For later periods in British history, archaeological discoveries made by amateurs are equally important, even though there is, for these periods, far more written evidence. The Vikings are a case in point. They are one of the most well known of ancient peoples, but are not usually viewed in a particularly positive light, largely due to historical evidence. The words 'rape' and 'pillage' are rarely very far away from the Vikings in the popular imagination, yet this perception only tells half the story. It is certainly the case that the Vikings, who originated in Scandinavia, raided the British Isles repeatedly from the late eighth century AD, with the earliest accounts coming from the *Anglo-Saxon Chronicle*. But the other side of the story, which is less widely known, is that many Vikings settled and ruled in parts of Britain, and gradually integrated with the local British population through marriage and other alliances. For many years, most of the evidence for these settlements came through place names, the most famous of which is probably Jorvik (modern York) where some of the best-preserved Viking remains in Britain can be found. Words known from local regional dialects also provide evidence for Viking settlers: for instance, the word *beck*, which is used in some parts of the country to mean stream, is known to come from the Old Norse word *bekkr*. Place names ending in 'by' and 'thorpe' are also Viking in origin.

Place-name evidence is useful because it can be a means of understanding where the Vikings established their communities. But place names do not tell us much about the daily lives of these Viking settlers. Much more evidence for this has begun to come to light in recent years, particularly through the discoveries of metal detector users. Some detectorists have discovered important Viking-age sites, such as Llanbedrgoch on the Isle of Anglesey in north Wales (see below, p. 113). Others have found metalwork which can provide a direct link to places where Viking-age settlements were established. This material is often not immediately recognisable as being Viking in origin, and has only recently been identified as such through the actions of dedicated local museum staff. These curators have built up a body of evidence over a number of years by encouraging local metal detectorists to report their finds and in some cases sell or donate their finds to regional museums. These discoveries hold the key to understanding the daily lives of an important group of people who settled on British soil, and from whom many of us directly descend.

The Vikings in East Anglia

Norfolk and Suffolk have one of the longest histories of local liaison work with metal detector users. Over the years, a vast quantity of information on local discoveries, particularly of metalwork, has been meticulously gathered together. Until her untimely death in 1997, much of what we know about these finds came from the painstaking work of Sue Margeson, whose research greatly aided our understanding of Viking settlement in the region.[18]

The Vikings were first recorded as coming to East Anglia in AD 866, where they set up bases for attacks on York. Just over ten years later East Anglia came under Viking control after a treaty had been signed with King Alfred. But, apart from historical sources and coinage, very little archaeological evidence survives, which is why finds made by amateur metal detector users are such an important source of information for this period. In East Anglia, finds have been recorded from all over the counties of Norfolk and Suffolk.

Much of the archaeological evidence found by detectorists is in the form of metalwork, more often than not worn on the body. For example, silver Thor's hammers have been found, including one from Lopham, Norfolk, and another from Leconfield, East Yorkshire. These were worn as amulets, or possibly charms. Thor was a popular Norse god, particularly associated with the weather and the sea, and they are sometimes found in Viking graves in the north of England or as accidental losses, which probably account for most of the East Anglian examples. Trefoil brooches, often made of copper or pewter, are also commonly found (fig. 81). Many have stylised leaf decoration or animal ornament which were very popular with the Vikings. Long pins were used to fasten cloaks, and strap-ends to decorate belts and prevent the ends from fraying, although, in the case of these finds, the organic part of the belt has long since decayed away.

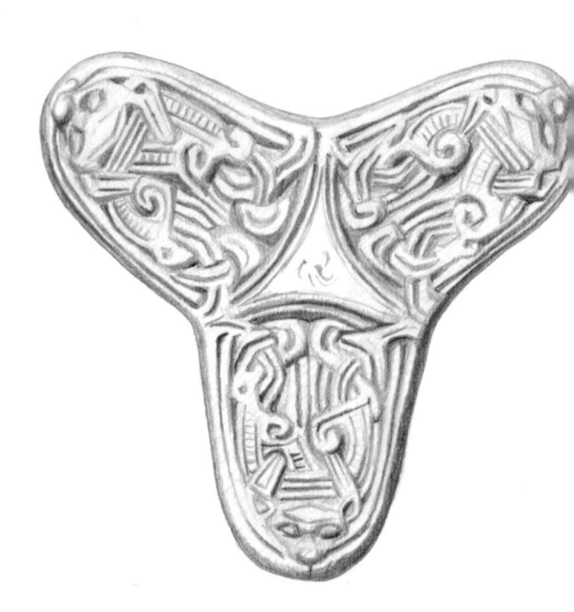

81 A sketch drawing of a trefoil brooch found in north Lincolnshire. These brooches are common finds of the Viking period in many parts of Britain.

By the eleventh century, two styles of artwork – known today as Ringerike and Urnes after places in Norway – become common on metalwork found in East Anglia. Unlike the earlier material which tends to be objects of personal adornment, many of the metal objects of this period are horse-fittings. These may be linked with new Viking raids which began in the late tenth century AD, and the conquest of England in 1016 by Cnut, who became king of England, Denmark, Norway and part of Sweden. Examples of this metalwork include Urnes-style mounts and strap-ends, which have a distinctive pattern of intertwined ribbons and snakes.

The Vikings in Lincolnshire

Another local museum curator, Kevin Leahy, has made huge strides in understanding the Viking period in Lincolnshire by systematically recording metal detector finds over the last twenty years.[19] It is known that a large invasion force of Vikings, often termed the Great Army, had set up camp at Torksey on the River Trent in the winter of AD 872–3, before moving south for the following year's campaign. We also know that the army divided into two in AD 877, with one part settling locally in Lincolnshire and the other taking over land in the East Midlands.

Our best evidence for the Viking settlement in Lincolnshire has always been the large number of Danish place names in the county and the Danish words used in the local dialect. In addition to this evidence, over 260 Viking and Anglo-Scandinavian objects have been recorded to date. As in East Anglia, much of this material consists of poor quality metalwork, often in the form of dress-fittings worn by women. These objects probably belonged to Vikings of relatively low social standing, who were either members of the Great Army or who followed on afterwards as settlers once the Vikings had established themselves in the area. They include trefoil brooches (see fig. 81), many of which are made of bronze, though occasionally some are of better quality with silver gilding and 'Borre' style decoration (characterised by interlocking geometric or zoomorphic elements). Stirrup strap mounts are also known from the area, as are other items of metalwork associated with horse harnesses and other trappings, and there are some examples of fittings from weapons such as sword scabbard mounts and pommels (see fig. 64). Vikings had also settled in coastal areas of Ireland, and there was a lively trade across the Irish Sea and around the British coast. Small quantities of Irish metalwork show that this trade stretched as far as Lincolnshire.

82 The prompt reporting of metal detected finds to the National Museums & Galleries of Wales by Archie Gillespie (shown here) and Peter Corbett led to the discovery of the site at Llanbedrgoch, Anglesey.

Many of these finds have come from rural sites, largely because metal detectorists in the area have favoured farmers' ploughed fields for the pursuit of their hobby. Often a single item from a particular location is all that is found, providing a fragment of evidence, but no more, for Viking settlement somewhere in the vicinity. Some sites, however, have produced finds in larger numbers, which might tell us where Vikings actually settled. In the future, it is hoped that these sites in particular can be investigated by archaeologists, which will provide more insights into the lives of these settlers in pre-Norman Lincolnshire.

The Vikings in Wales: Llanbedrgoch

Both Lincolnshire and East Anglia have produced large quantities of Viking period finds which can tell us a great deal about the lives of people during this period. In Wales, a rather different story can be told through one archaeological site which has been the subject of investigation by the National Museums & Galleries of Wales (NMGW) since 1994.[20]

The site of Llanbedrgoch on the Isle of Anglesey off the north Wales coast was originally discovered by two metal detectorists, Archie Gillespie and Peter Corbett (fig. 82). Back in 1992, Mr Gillespie and Mr Corbett reported the discovery of some coins and Viking weights. There was no obvious evidence in the landscape for any settlement in the area, so the NMGW, who had looked at the detectorists' finds, decided to conduct a geophysical survey and some trial excavations.

Llanbedrgoch has since proved to be one of the most important sites in Wales (figs 83–4). It consists of a fortified enclosure of about one hectare in size, inside which a number of activities – including farming and the manufacture of objects out of

83 *Left* The remarkable group of tenth-century burials found in ditch fill outside the defensive stone wall around the Viking Age enclosure at Llanbedrgoch, Anglesey.

84 *Above* Excavations in progress at the eastern side of Llanbedrgoch.

85 *Above inset* A small, early medieval iron bridle mount with red and yellow enamel inlay, one of the finest objects to come from the Llanbedrgoch excavations.

bronze, silver, tin and iron – have been identified. The site dates from the sixth to the eleventh centuries AD. This type of settlement is new to Wales because it is very rare to find all these activities taking place within a small enclosed space. The evidence comes in the form of a number of artefacts which have more than doubled the number of finds known from this period in Wales. The objects include hack-silver, which was used by the Vikings, alongside silver coinage, as a bullion form of currency; weights for measuring quantities of tradable commodities; and some examples of personal dress ornaments and decorative mounts, including a superb enamelled iron bridle mount of Irish type (fig. 85).

Outside the enclosure, another remarkable discovery of a rather different nature was excavated in 1998. This consisted of the remains of at least five well-preserved human skeletons. All seem to have been thrown into a ditch outside the walls in a very unceremonious fashion – in one case the adult male appeared to have had his hands tied behind his back. The orientation of the bodies is also significant, in all cases north to south. This goes against the standard Christian practice of east-west orientation. All this evidence makes it seem likely that they were not therefore buried by family, which would have been carried out in a far more respectful manner, but were instead the casualties of a violent act. One explanation to account for this discovery is that these people were murdered during a Viking raid on the site. Anglesey was subject to numerous raids in the tenth century, so it is not impossible that these individuals, who seem to have died no later than about AD 970, were the unfortunate victims of one of these raids. Another

The Cuerdale hoard

Metalwork hoards also add to our knowledge of the Viking period. The largest of these is the famous discovery from Cuerdale, Lancashire, in 1842 (fig. 86).[21] Found on the bank of the River Ribble, it consisted of about 8,600 items, mainly of silver, particularly coins and bullion, buried in a lead-lined chest. The whole find weighed some 40 kilograms. It is a hugely important find for understanding this period and is in fact the largest such hoard known from the whole of north-west Europe. Only Russia has produced hoards of similar size of this date.

As with many discoveries of this period (see Chapters 1 and 2), the circumstances surrounding this left something to be desired. It was found by one Thomas Marsden during repair work on the embankment of the river. He alerted the other workmen and they proceeded to dig up the hoard in a frenzy of excitement. The sheer size of the treasure would have made many of them feel, no doubt, as if this discovery could change their lives forever, and this was not a misguided view – it is estimated that the treasure would have been worth at least £500,000 in modern terms. At the time of burial, to have such a vast assemblage of material would have made the owner (or owners) the equivalent of multi-millionaires. However their excitement was short-lived because the local bailiff forced them to give up the find which was then removed to Cuerdale Hall nearby. For their troubles, the workmen were allowed to keep one coin each. If discovered today, and properly declared as Treasure (see p. 24), the finders would have been appropriately rewarded with the full market value of the find.

The hoard was further dispersed after a Treasure Trove inquest later that same year. It is known that some coins had, prior even to this, been taken away by a local coin dealer, who 'cherry-picked' some of the best and rarest examples. The whole find was split between a staggering forty-one British and foreign institutions, and at least 170 individuals, not all of whom are now known. However, the landowner, the Assheton family, and the British Museum retained the bulk of the hoard. Today, the national collection held at the British Museum has about 1,300 coins, some 740 other objects from the find, and the coins and objects owned by the landowner's family. It is unfortunate that the find was not kept together, but it nonetheless provides a key assemblage to understanding something about this period.

The hoard originally included about 7,500 coins. The bulk of these were Viking coins issued in Northumbria and East Anglia, but the hoard also included Anglo-Saxon coins, principally of Alfred the Great (AD 871–901) of Wessex, who ruled much of southern England. During his lifetime he attempted to defeat the Vikings and, although unsuccessful, he brought about peace through diplomacy. The main result of this was the creation of the 'Danelaw', the area of east England between the rivers Thames and Tees under Danish (Viking) rule, and within which English and Danes were treated equally. Also included in the hoard were 'Kufic' coins from all over the Islamic world, which at the time stretched from Spain through North Africa and the Middle East to Afghanistan.

The non-coin items consisted of ingots of silver, in various shapes and weights, and silver jewellery, much of which had been chopped up. This is often referred to as 'hack-silver' (or the German 'hacksilber'). Chopping up precious metal items was practised by different peoples at different times in the past, such as during the late Roman period, for a number of reasons. First, it created 'portable wealth': when large objects were cut up into smaller chunks, they could be more easily passed from hand to hand. This was often done at times when coinage – the usual source of portable

86 The Cuerdale hoard of Viking silver, Lancashire, buried *c.* AD 905–10.

wealth – was in short supply. This is an interesting way to treat precious objects, because it shows that the bullion value was more important than the objects' intended function – pieces of a silver brooch, for instance, were no longer any use for pinning a cloak, but were useful as currency. Additionally, it was a way of spreading wealth: a silver arm-ring made into hack-silver could be shared out between more people than if it were left whole. Smaller chunks were also easier to melt down and make into ingots of fixed weight or for recasting into other objects, for example jewellery.

Some of the jewellery was also whole, and the bulk of both intact jewellery and hack-silver consisted of arm-rings and brooches originating in Norse Ireland – parts of Ireland settled by Vikings. There were also some more exotic items, such as Scandinavian neck-rings, silver filigree (wire) jewellery from the east Baltic region and a fine Carolingian buckle from France. In contrast to the coins, there are only two items of Anglo-Saxon origin, a strap-end and a tiny mount.

Who owned Cuerdale and why was it buried?

The coins tell us that the hoard was buried between about AD 905 and 910. It is generally accepted that it belonged to more than one person because of its sheer size, but we do not know exactly who. One theory is that the owners were Vikings who had come from Ireland. In AD 902, Vikings had been expelled from Dublin, and some almost certainly fled to this area of Lancashire. The theory is that it constitutes a 'war chest' – a large amount of bullion gathered together with the intention of using it to raise a force to reclaim Dublin. This might explain why so much of the material in the hoard originated in Ireland, and also why so much of the coinage is new issues from the Viking mint at York. But it does not account for why it was never used – the only explanation for this would be that the owners fled or were killed before they could use it to mount their campaign.

Another similar proposition to that of a war chest is that Cuerdale belonged to a rich local leader who had buried his wealth as a type of bank: he could then hand out silver to his followers, hence maintaining his popularity. Perhaps he had already used some of the treasure in the past, but died or was killed before he was able to use the rest.

We shall probably never know the answers to these questions. Nevertheless, the Cuerdale hoard remains a find of huge importance for understanding the Viking period in Britain.

theory is that these are the bodies of Viking settlers or traders who were killed by locals and disposed of without the respect which would be bestowed on fellow Christians.

Toys were us: toys, trifles and miniatures in the Middle Ages

Date range: fourteenth to eighteenth centuries AD

In a similar manner to finds of the Viking period, recent metal detector discoveries have also modified our view of life during the Middle Ages. For many years, social historians thought that this was a time of little enjoyment for children, particularly in terms of toys, one of the principal things we associate with childhood today. Relatively recent discoveries in London completely reversed this view and demonstrated once again how new discoveries – and in this case the persistence of one amateur finder – can completely change our perception of the past.

During the 1980s in London, a huge boom in building led to vast amounts of new archaeological remains being uncovered. Under planning law, anyone constructing new buildings is obliged to pay for any resultant archaeological work because the work destroys archaeological remains when foundations are dug. In the City of London, in particular, the Museum of London was employing over one hundred full-time archaeologists to cope with all the new archaeological sites being exposed.

87 Excavations in the City of London during the 1980s. Archaeologists had to work fast to record and recover archaeological evidence of centuries of occupation.

Much of the work carried out in the 1980s was by necessity rescue work. The sheer volume of archaeological material in London is, not surprisingly, huge, with over 2,000 years of occupation from pre-Roman times until the present day forming deposits up to 10 metres thick below London's streets. Archaeologists did not have the luxury of being able to excavate the archaeology as thoroughly as they would have liked, as a fiercely competitive building industry sought to complete projects on time and within budget. Thus, in many instances, they were forced to plan and excavate literally as the diggers were moving in behind them, and huge amounts of material were removed without ever being properly investigated (fig. 87).

Despite the problems which archaeologists faced, many new and exciting archaeological sites were discovered, including the remains of Shakespeare's Globe Theatre and the Roman waterfront. In addition to these new sites, the excavations also led to the retrieval of a large number of ancient artefacts. Many of these were not found by professional archaeologists, but a local group of amateur metal detectorists, the Thames Mudlarks. Formed in 1980, this group is still one of the most active metal detector societies in the UK. Archaeologists and finds specialists at the Museum of London soon recognised the value to the excavations which the Mudlarks could bring, particularly given the rapidity by which material needed to be recovered. The speed by which soil was being shifted even meant that lorries containing spoil were often pursued by Museum staff and the detectorists, in order that more items could be recovered when the spoil was dumped at sites outside the capital (fig. 88).

88 Scanning the spoil heaps after soil from the City of London had been dumped outside the capital. Large numbers of important objects, including miniatures, were recovered which would otherwise have been lost.

Most of the Mudlarks took an interest in the larger objects which the Thames foreshore areas had preserved – for example, tools and weapons of all periods. However one Mudlark, Tony Pilson, decided to concentrate his efforts on recovering smaller, less easily recoverable objects, many of which were not recognisable at first. Pilson, over the course of two decades, amassed about 700 of these artefacts, both whole and fragmentary, and they were eventually acquired by the Museum of London, where they form an important part of the early London collections.

So what exactly was Tony Pilson finding? The bulk of Tony's finds date to the sixteenth to mid-eighteenth centuries, although the earliest examples date from about AD 1250, and they consist of tiny versions of everyday household objects. For this reason, they are often referred to as toys, although this may be somewhat misleading as they were not necessarily purely objects to be played with. A new publication of these finds describes them as 'toys, miniatures, and trifles', and these three terms are an apt way of describing them.[22]

89 A miniature birdcage, pewter, mid-seventeenth century AD.

Most of these objects seem to have been mass-produced, and are usually made of pewter, an alloy of tin, lead and copper in various combinations. The assemblage from London is easily the largest from any part of the British Isles. This is partly due to environmental factors because the muddy, damp conditions of the Thames foreshore provide an ideal environment for metals to be preserved. However, it is also likely that most were purchased and played with in London, with the rest distributed to other urban centres through trade. Many of these objects were undoubtedly manufactured by craftsmen with workshops in the city.

The range of toys, miniatures and trifles is quite spectacular. One category of object is household furniture. The Museum of London's collection includes miniature versions of a dining room cupboard, complete with hinged doors and the plate leant up against the shelved back. In this particular instance, the collection also has the 'flat pack' version of the cupboard, long before Ikea was even a twinkle in an entrepreneurial Swede's eye. This tells us that the metal alloy was poured into a flat mould and then bent into shape afterwards, which was probably done prior to sale. A stone mould of an early eighteenth-century watch confirms that this was the technique used.

Other household items include a turned three-legged stool and a birdcage (fig. 89) which even has the bird's feeder attached to the side. The interesting thing about these latter two objects is the fact that the full-sized versions of these objects have not survived (although some bird feeders have been found) which means that, because the miniatures were modelled on their full-sized counterparts, they are a very important social and historical document in their own right.

The kitchen is another household area which provided inspiration for these miniatures. Pigs on spits, fish on gridirons (fig. 90), and even frying pans with bubbling fat

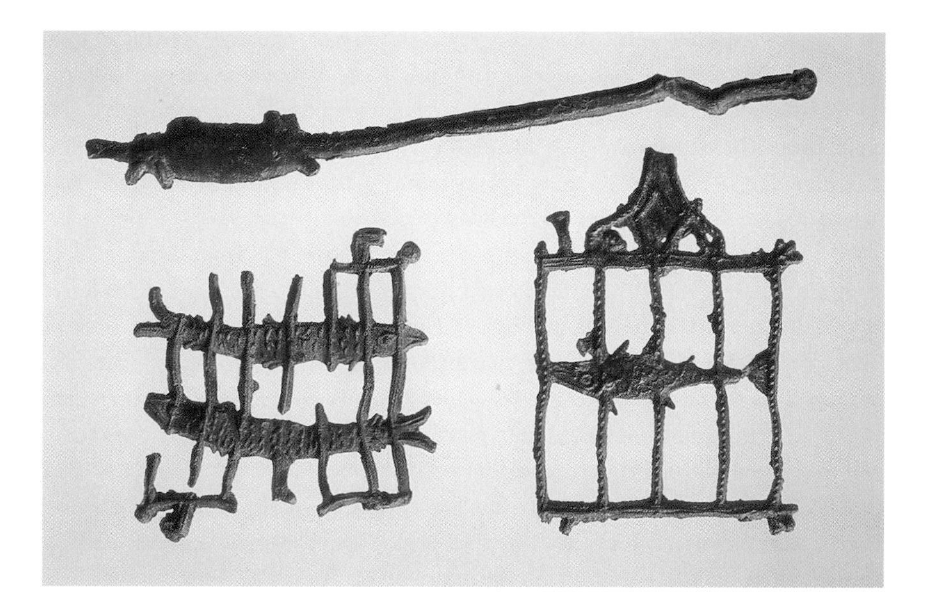

90 Miniature gridirons with fish and a pig on a spit, pewter, seventeenth century AD.

are just some of the objects which received the scaled-down treatment. For the dining element there are tiny pewter plates, porringers (small dishes for soup, porridge, and so on), spoons and ladles (fig. 91). Moving away from the interior of the home, there are miniature versions of horse-drawn carriages and even recognisably Elizabethan ships.

Not all miniatures were inanimate objects either: the Museum of London's collection includes a whole range of male and female figures with their own distinct period fashions, and even caricatures of local tradesmen with traces of the original paint still intact (fig. 92).

The most obvious use for these objects as children's toys is undoubtedly correct in most instances. Many would have been placed in early doll's houses, with all the

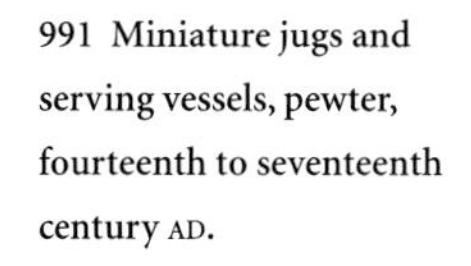

991 Miniature jugs and serving vessels, pewter, fourteenth to seventeenth century AD.

activities of the adult world able to be played out just as young children like to do today. Some of the toys also show evidence of use. There are cooking pots with sooting on them, which means they must have been placed on a fire; and we know that as a child Louis XIII of France (1610–43) used small pots for cooking (although these must have been a bit larger). A more worrying case of actual use is a toy cannon which had been fired; this could well have resulted in a nasty injury (fig. 93).

Adults too undoubtedly took great pleasure in these items. Duke Albrecht V of Bavaria (1528–79) is known to have commissioned a miniature version of his house with all its contents for his young daughter. However, upon seeing the final result he was so delighted that he decided to keep it for himself – we can only imagine how disappointed his poor daughter was as a result. But this story also tells us that these miniatures were highly prestigious items to have, and a means of demonstrating one's status and wealth, particularly as they served no practical function. It also seems that they could go out of fashion quickly. One example is a type of standing drinking cup known in miniature form, which was not a popular vessel type for very long in its full-scale version, falling out of use soon after its introduction in the early sixteenth century.

92 Miniature male and female pewter figures dressed in clothing typical of the late sixteenth century AD.

Toys are thus important social documents which no doubt gave as much pleasure to their original owners as they give to us today. If it were not for the actions of one dedicated finder, we would probably know far less about them. New categories of object continue to emerge through amateur discoveries which can provide similar insights into the lives of our ancestors. One example is dress accessories worn in Tudor England.

Forgotten fashions of the Tudors

Clothing fashions are an extremely important element of the way in which people express themselves in modern societies. This is nothing new – ever since humans first began pulling animal skins around themselves to keep warm, style of dress has been an important indication of ethnic background, social status and individuality. This chapter has already looked at a number of ways in which people in the past sought to modify their appearance (see pp. 102–10).

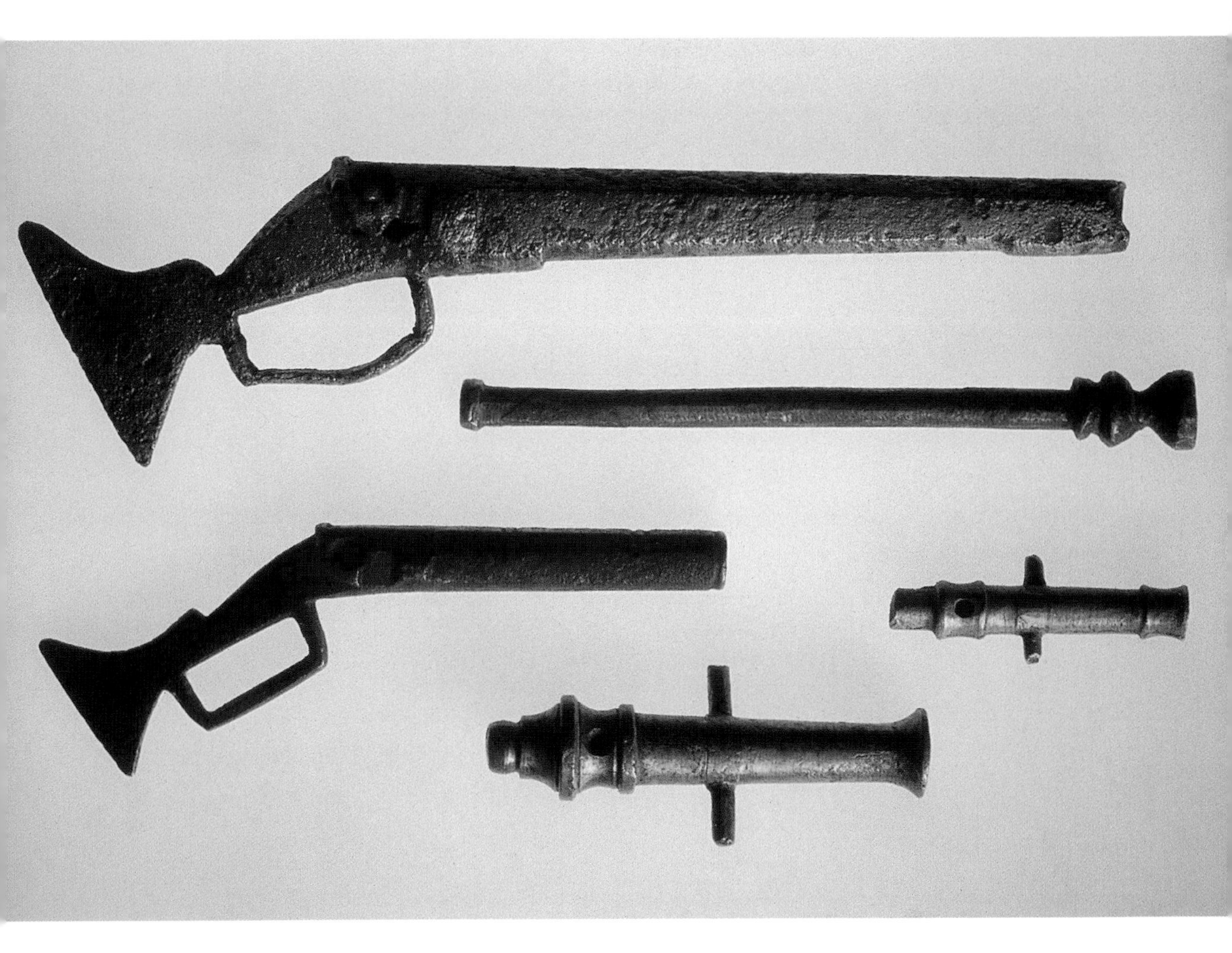

93 Miniature guns, pewter, late sixteenth to early seventeenth century AD.

One aspect of clothing, however, which we are likely to think much less about these days is how clothes fasten together. Nowadays, there are a number of ways in which this is done. Buttons and toggles are means by which two different elements of clothing, usually on the same garment, can be fastened. Belts and straps are used to tighten clothing so that it stays in place, with their adjustable nature allowing flexibility for different physiques. Buttons, toggles and belts, in one form or other, have a very long history, dating certainly from prehistoric times. Metal zips and inventions such as 'Velcro' are much more recent innovations.

In Tudor times, a rather different form of fastening was also used, in addition to buttons and belts. This is known as a dress-hook, and could range from low-quality cheap metal to very elaborate gold and silver objects set with gems (fig. 94). Since the Treasure Act came into force in 1997 (see p. 19), the number of these objects being reported has greatly increased. This is because they are often found by metal detector users as casual losses, whereas previously they were rarely found during archaeological excavations. Also, under old Treasure Trove law, small individual finds such as this were rarely reported, and in any case, it would have been hard to show that there had been an intention to recover them. The Portable Antiquities Scheme has also meant that the number of bronze and iron examples being recorded has greatly increased.

I myself first came across one of these curious objects on a rainy night at a metal detector group meeting in Dover (fig. 94, left). When shown to me, I knew that the object was made of silver and thus needed to be reported as potential treasure. But I

94 Two silver-gilt dress-hooks, used to hold garments together in Tudor times and as fashionable accessories.

was rather thrown by the distinctive hook at the top, and the cylindrical shape of the object. I only found out later that it dated to the sixteenth century, and that it was one of the more unusual forms of dress-hooks so far discovered.

Although these dress-hooks come in a variety of different forms, they all have three common elements. Each has a central body or plate as its main component; each has a hook; and most usually have either an opening in the central plate, or an additional bar attached to the back. They seem to have been used both as fastenings and as decoration. As fastenings, the method of attachment was relatively straightforward. To quote from a recent article on the subject:

'The bar on the back of the dress-hooks indicates that they were stitched permanently to a textile garment such as a cloak, or as an accessory such as a girdle. The hook was then put into a similarly worked piece of metal with a loop, a metal bar, a worked eyelet, or directly into another piece of fabric. This would allow the wearer either to keep two sides of a garment together, or to hold up long skirts in order to keep them clean.'[23]

Although the way in which they worked is fairly clear, it is not entirely certain which parts of the garments would have used these objects. Dress in Tudor times was very complicated, with a number of under and outer garments, and the fabrics used and the means of decorating these would have depended heavily upon social status. From studying historical sources, probate records, and some pictorial evidence, it seems most likely that dress-hooks were normally worn by women, probably wealthy members of the mercantile classes and the elite. One image in particular (fig. 95), which dates to the early 1530s, clearly shows a dress-hook in use by a lady to keep her skirts up when she is walking. This is unfortunately one of the few surviving contemporary images known which shows a dress-hook in direct use, so it is possible that they had other functions, for example to secure outer garments. But the high quality of the metalwork, often of good purity silver, often gilded and decorated with highly skilled work, also tells us that they had a decorative function. So in addition to holding up a lady's skirts, they were also an important dress accessory used to impress peers, for example at court events. By the late seventeenth century, however, they seem to have fallen out of use as a fashion accessory, just as fashions come and go in modern times.

95 Hans Holbein the Younger's drawing of *An English Lady Walking*, early 1530s. The front section of the lady's gown is attached to the girdle by a pair of dress-hooks.

Cap-hooks

As has been seen, it is thought that dress-hooks were almost certainly only used by women. For men, another class of hooked object seems to have been worn to impress others, this time on the cap rather than the skirt. Cap-hooks are another category of object which has begun to appear in larger numbers since the Treasure Act was introduced (fig. 96). These differ from dress-hooks because they have two elements to their construction rather than three: they do not have a bar or loop, but a simple plate and a hook or pin at the back so that they can be fixed to fabric.

These cap-hooks, like dress-hooks, are often silver-gilt, and some also have a livery function, such as an example from Raydon in Suffolk with an 'I' and two Tudor roses (see fig. 96, centre). Although limited in number, pictorial representations of Tudor men show these objects in use. Portraits dating to this time show cap-hooks being used to fasten together parts of the brim, or in order to fasten the brim itself to the crown of the cap. In both instances, the visible part of the small number of surviving cap-badges is decorative, so this was clearly another important reason why these were

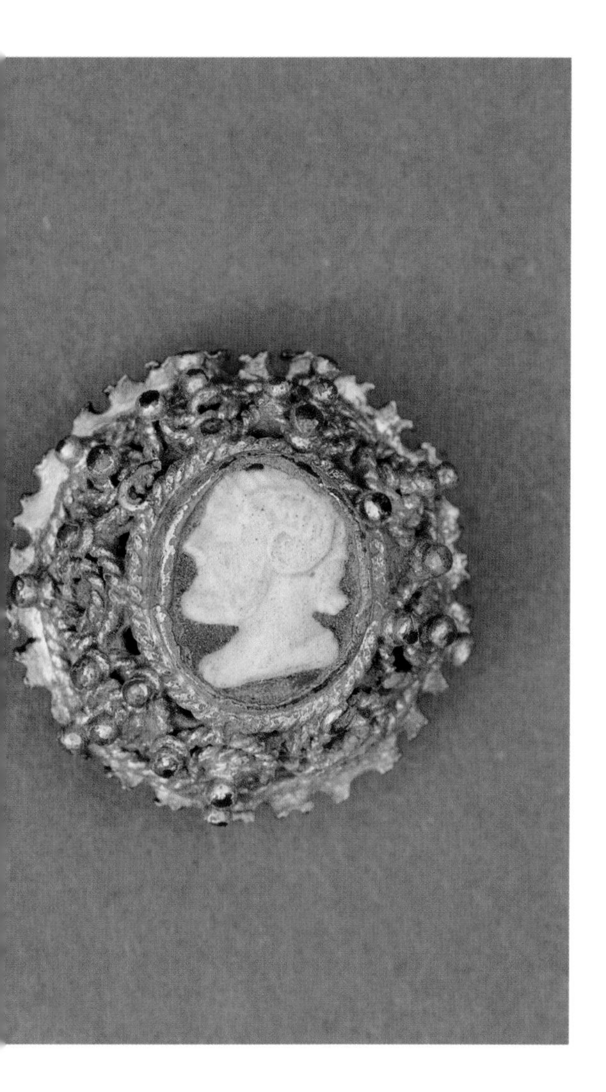

worn – they were once again a mark of social status. However, unlike the dress-hook, which seems to have fallen out of use, such cap-hooks continued to be used into modern times, with cap-badges, such as those worn by the military, still in use today.

Rings through the ages

'Whatever their shape, material or function . . . rings will always contain all the magic with which we ourselves endow them – expressions of our needs, our artistic ability and our technical skills.'[24]

All the objects discussed so far in this chapter have fallen in and out of use over the centuries, or were only used at one particular time in our past. Some types of object, however, allow us to trace whole histories of changing tastes and fashions across the centuries because they have been in constant use. Such an object is the finger-ring, which has been worn for thousands of years in all cultures across the world by men and women, adults and children. In many cases, the reason for wearing rings may have been nothing more than purely decorative. But the finger-ring is quite a particular type of jewellery which means that its function usually goes beyond simple aesthetics. Rings are one of the easiest items of jewellery to manufacture, and can be made from a wide variety of substances, from organic material such as amber to readily available metals such as copper, and less easily obtainable metals like gold or silver. This means that rings could be owned by people from all levels of society, and even the lower strata could sometimes afford rings made of precious substances because only small quantities of metal were needed to make them.

96 Silver-gilt Tudor cap-hooks: a six-spoked Catherine wheel inset with a flower-head, from Nettlestead, Suffolk (far left); engraved with a crowned 'I' between two Tudor roses, from Raydon, Suffolk (centre); with pierced and filigree decoration and a cameo portrait of Jupiter Ammon, from Kingerby, Lincolnshire (far right).

The finger-ring itself is symbolic for a variety of reasons. The eternal nature of a circle, with no beginning or end, imbues finger-rings with an everlasting quality. Rings are often hard to remove once placed on the hand, which adds to this feeling of eternity. Rings are also visible to both the wearer and anyone with whom the wearer had contact (unless gloves are being worn), as hands are one of the principal ways in which people express themselves. The robust nature of rings also gives them a potential longevity beyond one lifetime; they are often handed down as heirlooms, providing a particularly strong symbolic link with predecessors.

In the past, rings were worn on all parts of the finger and thumb, and often over gloves – very large rings therefore did not necessarily belong to individuals with enormous hands. Equally, very small rings did not necessarily belong to children. Portraits from the sixteenth century even show rings sewn into sleeves, cuffs and hats, or suspended from chains or cords, such was their importance to the wearer.[25] There was also at many periods a strict code which governed the wearing of rings by the different sexes and social classes – the sumptuary laws of the fourteenth century, for instance, limited the wearing of precious metal rings to the higher classes. Rings could also be worn on toes as well as fingers.

Some rings served practical functions, when it was important that they were close to the body for safety. Roman key rings, used to open caskets, are a good example. Other practical uses included personal signet rings (see below), or rings which had a miniature watch set into them. Other rings were worn for spiritual reasons and as amulets (see opposite).

Personal signs

Rings have been used since Roman times to provide a shorthand for specific personal family or business names, usually for practical use to make marks. Intaglios were stones in which an inscription or device was cut in reverse, allowing an impression to be made in wax or similar substances. In the Roman period, intaglios might contain the symbol of a pagan god, such as a wine cup for Bacchus, or, from the fourth century AD, the Chi-Rho Christian monogram. Some also had the initials of personal names. Throughout the medieval period, Roman intaglios were often re-used in rings, because their antiquity was no doubt seen to enrich them with a special significance.

Signet rings continued to be worn during the medieval period, and it was standard practice to use them for making impressions in wax to seal letters or documents. Heraldic devices and merchants' marks are the commonest types. At some periods when the supply of stones could not keep pace with demand, metal bezels engraved with these devices became common. Sometimes badges were combined with a personal motto, such as on a ring from Raglan, Monmouthshire, which dates to the fifteenth century (fig. 97). This is a massive gold ring, probably worn over a glove, which has a heraldic device in the form of a lion *passant*[26] on a bed of flowers, the legend 'feythfoull to yow' ('faithful to you') and the letters 'W A'.

97 The Raglan ring, Monmouthshire, fifteenth century AD, one of the largest signet rings ever discovered.

Signet rings continued to be popular in the Renaissance and early modern times, and even today remain a very popular ring type, particularly amongst men. My father possessed for many years a signet ring with a Star of David on the bezel, which he wore simply because he liked the design, not because he is Jewish. Although no longer used to mark wax seals, these types of rings are the direct descendant of medieval and Roman signets. Rings with personal names, usually cheaply produced and gold-plated, are also popular in Britain today and represent a continuation of the desire for rings with personal marks.

Religion and magic

Finger-rings have been worn for centuries for religious and superstitious reasons. The most famous fictional example of a ring with magic powers is in J.R.R. Tolkien's *Lord of the Rings* where the ring is central to a story of the struggle between good and evil. The small size of rings, the intimacy with the wearer, the ease by which symbols or stones on rings are visible to others, all help to explain why they have a particular association with religion and magic.

Snake rings from the Roman period are very common finds in Britain (fig. 98). In

The power of gemstones

Stones set in finger-rings were from ancient times supposed to offer protection against different ailments, or were talismanic for certain social conditions and events which could befall one. Some of the properties of different stones are listed as follows:

Amethyst – protected from drunkenness (Classical period)
Sapphire – protected from poison (Classical period); expelled envy and detected fraud and witchcraft (medieval period)
Emerald – protected against treachery (Classical period); beneficial against epilepsy and eye complaints (medieval period)
Garnet – protected from accidental injury (Classical period)
Amber – thought to have restorative powers against toothache and headache (Classical period)
Lapis lazuli – thought to improve sexual prowess (Classical period)
Diamond – protected against nightmares and gave courage (medieval period)
Turquoise – helped to prevent falls whilst riding (medieval period); also known as the 'compassionate' jewel as its colour supposedly changes according to the health of the wearer.
'Toadstone' (fossilised teeth of the *Lepidotes*) – thought to protect against poison and help alleviate kidney disease (medieval period)

the Classical world the snake was perceived as being highly beneficial, and was associated with healing, rebirth and regeneration.[27] The form of the snake also lent itself easily to being formed into rings, which could range from very simple copper loops with a triangular head and a rounded tail, to elaborate gold examples with twisted bodies. When Christianity became the principal religion in Britain from the early medieval period, the snake fell out of use because of its negative association with the story of Adam and Eve, but was revived in the nineteenth century when it once again became a symbol of eternity.

Classical deities were often depicted on rings as a way of bringing good fortune to the wearer. Mars, the god of war, and the personification of Victory were popular with Roman soldiers for obvious reasons. In medieval times, Christian symbolism took over, with rings made to contain relics of saints and then, increasingly, 'iconographic' rings, which had saints engraved on the bezel. Popular saints included St Margaret (similar to the Roman Minerva, protector of women in childbirth) and St Christopher, associated with the prevention of sudden death and the patron saint of travellers. The latter both reflect a direct attempt to avert inherent dangers of two of the most hazardous activities of medieval life, giving birth and travelling on public highways. Related to St Christopher is the use of turquoise as settings on rings, because it was supposed to help prevent accidents whilst riding – other stones were thought to have different properties in Classical and later times (see box p. 129). Gems were also sometimes engraved with magical symbols or astrological signs. Stones were sometimes set so that they touched the skin, in order that the properties they supposedly possessed might be more effective.

98 A Roman snake ring from the Backworth hoard, Northumberland, second century AD. Snake rings are relatively common metal detector finds – the snake was identified in Roman times with healing, rebirth and regeneration.

Some rings contained inscriptions which were also thought to bring luck. In the Classical period, Latin inscriptions on rings were usually very simple, for example a person's name followed by *vivas* ('may you live'), or phrases such as *utere felix* ('use this happily'). In the medieval period, biblical quotations were common. One example is found on thirteenth-century rings, which were inscribed 'IESUS AUTEM TRANSIENS PER MEDIUM MILLORAM IBAT' ('But He passing through the midst of them went His way') and designed to help secure possessions as the phrase was taken to mean safe passage through thieves. Rings were also engraved with magic charms in the hope of warding off ailments which were thought to be the work of evil spirits – 'ANANYZAPTA', for example, was a charm against epilepsy.

Some rings had a specific more practical function in religion (fig. 99). The best example of this is the post-medieval decade ring. Such rings had ten knobs sticking out from the hoop, and sometimes also figures of saints engraved on them. These fulfilled the same function as rosary beads and were used to count off prayers.

Religious and 'magic' rings are not so commonly worn these days, but the tradition does continue to some extent in the form of 'birthstone' settings. Even if the wearer does not necessarily know the perceived properties of the stone as worn, such stones are still meant, in a rather diluted fashion, to bring the wearer good luck.

LOVE AND MARRIAGE

The most common finger-ring worn today is the wedding ring – a simple band of gold, or sometimes other metals or alloys, worn by both men and women on the third finger of the left hand (or the right hand in many continental countries). It is a symbol of the eternal nature of the wedding bond, and a social signal of unavailability to potential suitors. The other common ring is the engagement ring, only worn by women, often placed before the wedding ring on the same finger, and usually set with one or more gemstones. Although solitaire settings are common in the twenty-first century, multiple settings have been fashionable in the past and could well become so again.

In the past, wedding rings and rings symbolising a declaration of love were also common, although it is often less possible to distinguish the exact intention of the finger-ring as found – in some cases, it may have been an indication of allegiance or close friendship rather than romantic involvement. Clasped hands rings, known as the *fede* (from the Latin for 'faith') ring in medieval times (fig. 100) and *dextrarum iunctio* ('clasped right hands') rings in the Roman period (fig. 101), are examples of this potential ambiguity. Interlocking hoops or 'gimmel' rings of medieval and later times were also both marriage and allegiance rings. These were made as a pair, and then separated out from each other and exchanged. More clear-cut marriage rings, however, were portrait rings with facing male and female busts; these were common in the late Roman period.

99 *Above* A medieval silver-gilt finger-ring from the Hackleton area, Northamptonshire, with an engraving of a saint, which may be Barbara, on the bezel.

100 A medieval gold finger-ring from Gedney, Lincolnshire, fifteenth century AD. On one side of the hoop are two hands ending in a lover's knot; on the other is a rather worn amatory inscription, beginning with 'A M O . . .'.

Another development in the medieval period was the so-called 'posy' ring, which is a relatively common metal detector find. These rings had simple declarations of love on the inner or outer side of the hoop. An example of a typical medieval inscription is 'MON CUER AVEZ' ('you have my heart'). The word 'posy' is derived from the

French *poésie* (poetry) and was used from the sixteenth century, by which time inscriptions were often in rhyming couplets and invariably on the inside, hidden to all but the wearer.

Wedding rings and rings given as declarations of love is the one area of ring history which crosses all the boundaries of social class and status. Such was the importance of the wedding ring at some points in time that it even came under state control. During the Victorian period, the Wedding Rings Act of 1852 stipulated that all rings should be hallmarked as a guarantee of quality. And during the Second World War, when gold became scarce and its use needed to be rationed, goldsmiths were ordered to restrict the size of rings to only 2 pennyweights, be plainly designed, 9 carat and bear a government approved mark.[28]

101 A Roman gold finger-ring from Bowerchalke, Wiltshire, late fourth century AD. The bezel depicts two clasped right hands (*dextrarum iunctio*), a symbol of allegiance or marriage.

Death and memorial

> 'I judged him to be a bachelor from the frayed condition of his linen, and he appeared to have sustained a good many bereavements; for he wore at least four mourning rings, besides a brooch representing a lady and a weeping willow at a tomb with an urn on it. I noticed too that several rings and seals hung at his watch-chain, as if he were quite laden with remembrances of dear departed friends.'[29]

Rings associated with death and remembering those who have passed away only became common in post-medieval times. *Memento mori* ('in remembrance of death') rings were worn to remember the person who had died and as a reminder to the living of mortality (fig. 102). Good examples of the memorial ring are those worn by the followers of Charles I after his death in 1649, which contained a miniature portrait of the dead king.

Such rings were often distributed in accordance with a person's will after death. It was possible that the list of people receiving these could be quite long, and thus it could be very expensive for the estate of the person who passed away. Occasionally, these mourning rings contained a relic of the deceased, which came in the form of hair set within glass in the bezel or as a braided band around the hoop.

During the First World War, rings were often the only personal item which soldiers kept on them and so the only token they could leave to their sweetheart or family. Soldiers without rings even made them out of wire, shrapnel or cartridges.

Rings associated with death and memorial are no longer worn these days, although imagery such as the skull and crossbones is sometimes found on rings worn by cult fashion movements such as Goths of the 1980s. Although the practice of leaving a sum of money in a will to have remembrance rings made has now died out, rings such as wedding or engagement rings are still traditionally passed down through the family, for example from a grandmother to granddaughter.

Small things remembered?

This chapter has looked at a whole range of 'small things forgotten', tiny remnants of the past which, when pieced together, can evoke stories and images of the everyday lives of ancient peoples. A huge debt is owed to the amateur finders of all these fragments of heritage, and also to the dedicated museum professionals and archaeologists who have taken it upon themselves to understand the stories that these small objects relay.

All the finds discussed in this chapter have been reported by responsible members of the public who have looked beyond the potential rewards to the wider picture painted by these pieces and shared their discoveries with others. The next chapter discusses those who have in contrast sought to keep pieces of the past purely for their own gain.

102 Gold and enamel finger-ring with an inscription 'Hodie mihi cras tibi' ('Today it is me but tomorrow it will be you'). From Rushton, Cheshire, late sixteenth or early seventeenth century AD.

5

Our Precious Past

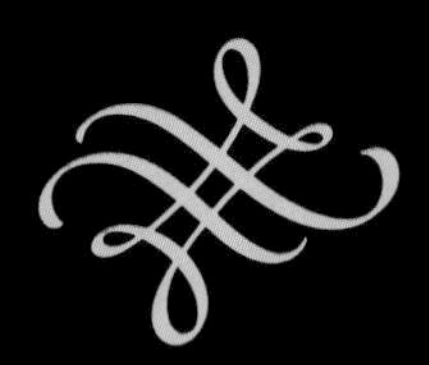

Introduction

> 'Unprovenanced antiquities, ripped from their archaeological context without record . . . can tell us little that is new. The opportunity is thereby lost for them to add to our understanding of the past history and prehistory of the regions from which they come, or to our perception of the early development of human society'.[1]

It is a simple fact that, without the cooperation of the public, museums in Britain would not have the opportunity to acquire and display treasure finds. There are many ways in which treasure and other archaeological discoveries are made (see Chapter 2), but over 90 per cent of treasure items are unearthed during amateur metal detecting or during the course of building and agricultural work – all by ordinary people going about their daily lives or pursuing their hobby. Well-reported discoveries provide a far greater depth of knowledge about our past; the vast majority of finds so far discussed fall into this category. The good reporting of some finders has even been formally recognised by the wider archaeological world, for example Phil Shepherd and Mike Chambers are both recipients of British Archaeological Awards (see pp. 99–102). Other finders have behaved responsibly by recognising the importance of involving professional archaeologists in their discoveries, such as Eric Lawes, the finder of the Hoxne hoard (see p. 78), and Archie Gillespie and Peter Corbett, the original finders of the Viking site of Llanbedrgoch, Anglesey (see p. 113).

When treasure discoveries are made, they are obliged to be reported by law, otherwise finders could face a hefty fine or even imprisonment. But laws are not always obeyed and some discoveries of treasure are never declared and reported in the correct manner. The reasons for this will vary. Some archaeological sites, such as the Roman temple at Wanborough (see below, p. 142) have been deliberately targeted by unscrupulous treasure hunters, who have stolen archaeological finds and sold them on to equally unscrupulous antiquities dealers. In other cases, amateurs might make discoveries when they are metal detecting on land without permission. This may not necessarily happen deliberately, for example a detectorist may wander onto an area of land adjacent to that where he or she does have permission to search. If finds are then made, the finder, on realising his or her mistake, might not declare finds in fear of reprisals, and might approach an antiquities dealer willing to purchase material 'with no questions asked'. Alternatively, some finders are simply suspicious of authority or are ignorant of the Treasure law, and either keep their finds without realising their importance or sell them to a dealer.

The scale of the problem of these illicitly recovered antiquities is very difficult to assess. By its very nature, we are dealing with the intangible: the actual number of objects lost to archaeology can never be measured accurately. Working in the museum world, one often hears rumours of alleged new discoveries, but more often than not the artefacts never see the light of day. If objects do subsequently appear, it is even rarer to know from where exactly they were originally looted, unless an archaeological site is known to have been targeted. The Roman temple at Wanborough, where large-scale looting is known to have taken place, is very much the exception to the rule. Not knowing the provenance of looted objects greatly decreases their value as archaeological material: the vital importance of archaeological context, which underpins much of what we can sensibly say about important discoveries, has been a recurring theme throughout this book. Conversely, it throws the responsible reporting and recording of findspots by individuals such as Kevan Halls, the finder of the Winchester hoard (see p. 59), into even sharper focus. As was seen in the discussion of that particular find, without knowledge of the findspot it is highly unlikely that anyone would have considered some items in this find – particularly the unusual torcs – to have come from Hampshire.

Three case studies of the illegal recovery of antiquities are provided below, each with a rather different story to tell. The first case – the site of Snettisham in Norfolk – is a mixed tale, beginning with responsible reporting which eventually provided us with arguably the most important assemblage of precious objects ever recovered from Iron Age Britain. But the tale ends with a contrasting story of a further set of material which could have been the key to understanding the site but is probably now lost for ever. The second is an example of large-scale looting of an important archaeological site, the Roman temple at Wanborough in Surrey. The only positive aspect of this sorry tale, and small consolation, is the role Wanborough played in the eventual changes to the Treasure law in England and Wales. Finally, the third tale of the Salisbury hoard is essentially a tale of hope. What looked initially like the destruction and loss of a highly important set of archaeological material led in the end, through the actions of a tenacious archaeologist, to something approaching a well-understood archaeological site.

Snettisham: 'the one that got away'

Dates of discovery: 1948, 1950, 1990; date of burial: mid-first century BC *to first century* AD

Snettisham in Norfolk is undoubtedly one of the key sites of British prehistory (fig. 103). Occupying a wooded hillside near the north-west Norfolk coast close to Hunstanton, it first began to reveal its secrets in 1948 when five torcs were unearthed during ploughing. Torcs, worn around the neck, are arguably the most evocative and symbolically charged items of Iron Age material culture, and of undoubted significance to pre-Roman societies across huge areas of north-west Europe (their importance has already been discussed elsewhere – see p. 62). The highly decorated and elaborate gold examples from Snettisham represent the pinnacle of Iron Age craftsmanship and artistic endeavour.

More torcs emerged in the 1950s, also through ploughing, including the so-called 'Great torc', seen by many as *the* symbol of the British Iron Age. More excavations at the site soon followed, but did not lead to any significant new discoveries, and many thought that there was nothing more to be found. However, in 1990 a local metal detectorist, Wing Commander Charles Hodder, gained permission to detect on the site, and soon made a spectacular discovery. He found a huge deposit of torcs still *in situ* – previous finds having been scattered by the plough – and reported his discovery to the landowner. Dr Ian Stead, then Deputy Keeper of Prehistoric and Romano-British Antiquities at the British Museum, was informed of the discoveries and

mounted a rescue excavation. The survey and excavation work led to the recovery of a further five hoards, all of which had been buried in 'nests' in discrete burial pits. Each deposit contained torcs of various type and metals, some broken and some repaired. In addition, some imported Iron Age gold coins, dating to the early second century BC, and some items of scrap metal and ingots were recovered from the ploughsoil, although they were probably originally in the pits as well. Charles Hodder behaved admirably in only claiming a Treasure Trove reward for his initial discovery.

There are at least twelve hoards known to date from Snettisham. Hoard L is one of the richest and deepest deposits, and showed considerable care over its burial (fig. 104). A deep shaft had been sunk, with the most elaborate gold torcs placed at the bottom of the pit on top of each other; an additional layer of soil was then added before a further set of torcs was placed on top of each other and the shaft sealed. The ability to excavate torcs *in situ*, which had come about as the result of prompt reporting on the part of Charles Hodder, was the first time this had been possible in the UK or indeed Europe (figs 105–6). This type of detailed contextual information about the site makes Snettisham unique.

103 Snettisham, Norfolk, one of the few high points in the landscape in this part of Britain.

104 *Right* One of the hoards of torcs found at Snettisham, Norfolk (Hoard L), still *in situ*.

The question which follows is why were the torcs deposited in this manner, in this series of burial pits? Before this can be addressed it is necessary to understand how the objects might have been used before they were buried. The torcs were made of a variety of metal alloys and in a number of different ways, from simple twisted wire torcs to very elaborate ones with decorated terminals and many twisted wire strands, the most magnificent of which is the 'Great torc'. Some show evidence of repair, necessary because opening and closing them to put them on and take them off had weakened the metal. This evidence is important for a number of reasons. Firstly, it tells us that many – if not all – the torcs in the deposits had actually been used as necklaces. This might seem obvious, but if the torcs had shown no signs of actual use, then it would have implied that they might have been made specifically for the burial act itself. Secondly, it shows that they were repeatedly taken on and off, which implies that they were not being worn all the time. In modern times, it is rare for necklaces to be worn constantly, but in the Iron Age torcs may well have been worn for long periods and not taken off until the wearer died. Some of the torcs in the Snettisham hoards might have only been worn once, but the repaired ones at least may have been worn only occasionally. Perhaps this means that they were used just for special occasions – maybe ceremonial or religious – not unlike the vestments and regalia worn by church officials or royalty in modern times which relate to specific rituals and ceremonies. The high quality of the workmanship on some of the torcs would also fit with this proposition.

This brings us to the question of why these torcs were buried at Snettisham and, effectively, abandoned. Reasons for burial of precious objects – already discussed in Chapter 2 – tend to relate either to the sacred, such as burial as part of a ritual, or to the profane, such as burial for safekeeping, and both of these reasons have been put forward in the case of Snettisham. Some argue that the careful deposition in pits over

105 Archaeological planning of one of the torc deposits at Snettisham, before the hoard was excavated.

a period of perhaps fifty to a hundred years was enacted either to placate the gods, if some catastrophic event had befallen the community, or as an attempt to influence them and thus shape future events. 'Sacrifice' of precious objects was a way of creating a relationship with the gods in the hope of a return – not necessarily specified – in the future. In addition, some of the torcs may have been deliberately broken for similar reasons. The position of Snettisham on high ground also adds weight to the idea that this was an important ritual site, as other similar precious metal finds of this period, from Winchester and Leicestershire, are on similarly exposed high areas (see pp. 59 and 65). The parallels between these sites, away from settlement and at high points in the landscape overlooking large areas, is one of the most exciting fields of research currently taking place in British archaeology.

Alternatively, more pragmatic reasons might explain the careful burial of these precious metal hoards. Some have argued that Snettisham could have been a place where the local community stored its wealth, a little like a primitive bank. In this scenario, the location would have been known only to that community, with precious metals removed as necessary to use perhaps for forming alliances with neighbouring tribes, marriage dowries, or to be recast and reworked into other precious metal items. An argument in

106 Controlled metal detecting at Snettisham.

favour of this is that, in addition to the torcs, the site has also produced gold bullion in the form of ingots and coins, which, it is alleged, have no other function than exchange or recycling. Suggesting that the site represents such a bullion store does not however preclude it from having a ritual significance as well – Snettisham could have served a variety of different functions within the local community.

The torcs and other finds from Snettisham are preserved and displayed in Norwich Castle Museum and the British Museum where they are enjoyed by millions of visitors every year. The same cannot be said, however, of a further hoard – frequently termed the 'Bowl hoard' – which has unfortunately probably been lost forever.

The 'Bowl hoard'

Ian Stead firmly believed that his survey had been as thorough as possible across the whole of the accessible areas of the Snettisham site. But a year or so after his excavations were completed, rumours began to circulate that another hoard had been found on the site, and it was even suggested in some quarters that this was located below one of the burial pits which the British Museum had excavated. This hoard, which has become known as the 'Bowl hoard', or in Stead's own words as 'the one that got away', is said to have consisted of over 6,000 silver coins buried in a silver bowl, with a further set of 500 gold coins and ingots, buried underneath the bowl in the same burial pit.[2] The coins are reported to have been of local types generally associated with the Iceni tribe, but also of types usually found in the Lincolnshire and Leicestershire region, attributed to the Corieltauvi (similar to the coins in fig. 39). Many of these coins have been seen by those with connections to the antiquities trade, but the bowl has never surfaced in all the years since it was supposedly discovered.

The loss of the 'Bowl hoard' to archaeology is extremely significant and deeply sad. The whole find was sold after discovery, with the contents divided up among a number of different antiquities dealers, which makes the task of reconstructing the contents of the find very difficult (although some have attempted to do so). This was an illegal act on the part of both the finders, who should have declared the find as possible Treasure Trove, and the dealers, who should not have purchased stolen goods.

If the 'Bowl hoard' really had been found at Snettisham, as rumours strongly suggest, then it is a very different type of deposit to the others known from the site and now in the public domain. The coins are from a later period than the torcs and coins preserved in Norwich and London, as they date mostly to the late decades of the first century BC and the early first century AD. This means that the site was potentially in use somewhat longer than had previously been thought, and may even have overlapped with the invasion of Britain by the Romans in AD 43. In addition, if there really was a silver bowl in which these coins had been buried, this also makes it a very different type of deposit to the others known from the site.

We shall probably never know the true nature of the 'Bowl hoard', and this constitutes a very damaging loss to our heritage. The only comfort is the fact that the majority of the finds from the site have been properly excavated. The same cannot be said of the Romano-British temple at Wanborough in Surrey, where only a fraction of finds known from the site have ever been recovered. The story of Wanborough, which had a key part to play in the reform of the treasure laws, is told below.

107 Wanborough Roman temple, Surrey. This photograph shows the most damaged part of the site, after excavation, of all the material disturbed by illicit metal detecting. Part of the hedgerow had to be removed as it had been killed by treasure hunters undermining it from both sides.

The battle of Wanborough temple

> 'No-one who claims an interest in the past could possibly view the destruction at Wanborough with anything but horror, or fail to recognise that there is a need for changes in the law.'[3]

The 'Bowl hoard' from Snettisham is an example of an important find which is known to have disappeared from a well-known archaeological site. It is probable, though, that the rest of the torc burials from this key site have been recovered and reported properly, which means that it is possible to study and enjoy these finds as a key part of the holdings of both Norwich Castle Museum and the British Museum.

Sadly this cannot be said of the discoveries from another important site, that of the Romano-British temple at Wanborough in Surrey. For some archaeologists, this site still encapsulates their misgivings about the antiquities laws in England and Wales which they regard as being inadequate, although most would accept that the Treasure Act is a major step forward in the right direction (see Chapter 1).

The story of Wanborough begins back in 1983. Two metal detectorists were searching along a lane in Surrey. They discovered some gold and silver Iron Age and Republican coins which they declared to Guildford Museum. The Museum requested that the location of the site remain a secret, but at a coroner's Treasure Trove inquest in 1984 the exact location of the site was unfortunately given out. This information was used by unscrupulous detectorists from different parts of the country, and publicity for the site in the Press led to yet more detectorists visiting it. These individuals, often working under cover of darkness, dug huge holes and even destroyed parts of an ancient hedgerow in their quest for treasure (fig. 107). Showing no regard for the archaeological remains and largely avoiding the attention of the local police – although some were arrested – these 'nighthawks' removed a mass of material. This material, which consisted of thousands of Iron Age and Roman coins and a number of religious objects such as sceptre handles and head-dresses, soon began to flood the antiquities market, and occasionally even resurface to this day. Some of it was seized by the police, but the vast majority has disappeared into private collections and will probably only re-emerge when these collections are sold. The British Museum was able to acquire some of the finds seized, which consisted of over 1,000 coins from the site. These constitute one of the most important assemblages of gold and silver coinage of the late Iron Age in southern Britain (fig. 108), but are only a proportion of

108 A small sample of Iron Age silver coins from Wanborough, recovered by the police and now preserved in the British Museum (not to scale).

the total number of coins found at the site, which is estimated at between 5,000 and 7,000 pieces,[4] although others even put the figure as high as 20,000.[5] The archaeological context for this mass of material will never be able to be recovered.

The Surrey Archaeological Society was powerless to stop the looting of this important local site. But they did manage to raise the funding and resources to mount an excavation, and a full rescue dig commenced in 1985.[6] It lasted for four months and, although the site had been very badly damaged, archaeologists were able to recover finds which had escaped the attentions of the looters (figs 109–10). They were also able to establish that the site was that of a square Romano-Celtic temple, which was built in the second century AD and continued to be used into the second half of the fourth century AD. Further excavation work also took place in 2000, once again instigated by further looting of the site, and this revealed an earlier Romano-Celtic circular temple. Both this discovery and the looted finds from it showed that the site had first been used in the late Iron Age (the late first century BC).

109 A priest's head-dress from Wanborough, in the form of a series of chains linked to a cap with a five-spoked wheel. It is thought that the wheel is a solar symbol, which may mean that the temple was dedicated to a Celtic form of the Roman sun god, Jupiter.

The destruction of the site at Wanborough had far-reaching effects beyond the physical loss of archaeological evidence from a Romano-Celtic temple. Resultant relations between both professional and amateur archaeologists and metal detectorists hit an all-time low, and there were calls from many sections of the archaeological profession for the hobby to be banned. But, as with football hooligans whose actions do not reflect the football-supporting body as a whole, most detectorists are law-abiding citizens with a genuine interest in the past. Over the next two decades, both detectorists and archaeologists therefore sought to build bridges and find ways of working with each other. These efforts eventually led to the establishment of new Treasure legislation and the Portable Antiquities Scheme in 1997 (see Chapter 2). Nevertheless, the illegal removal of antiquities continued, one of the most high profile cases being that of the Salisbury hoard.

The Salisbury hoard: a true archaeological detective story

Unlike Wanborough, knowledge about an important prehistoric site near Salisbury came about through rather different channels. In this case, none of the original finds were declared to the authorities, and establishing the way in which the material was divided represents a true archaeological detective story on the part of a former British Museum curator.[7]

The first indication that an interesting discovery had been made came in the summer of 1988. A London antiquities dealer, Lord Alistair McAlpine, showed Dr Ian Stead of the British Museum twenty-two bronze miniature shields, in various states of preservation, which he immediately recognised as being highly unusual and probably of Iron Age date. However, the shields presented the Museum with a problem: although they were clearly important, they did not have a good provenance – it was not clear how or where they had been found. In most cases, the Museum will not acquire such material, but in this case, because the material was so unique, an exception was made. This demonstrates the difficulties often faced by museums which have to weigh up the pros and cons of purchasing archaeological material, the like of which may never be seen again, against the problems of not having a proper context for the find. However, it has to be borne in mind that information relating to a findspot can emerge at a later date which means that material will sometimes be acquired, in very exceptional circumstances, in the hope that this occurs. In this instance, this proved to be the case.

110 Two sceptre handles from Wanborough. Although their exact function is unclear, they were probably used by temple priests during rituals.

Soon after the British Museum acquired these shields, rumours began to circulate of the discovery of a massive hoard consisting of 1,500 bronze objects which apparently included miniature shields. One of the accounts of the find came from a man with whom Dr Stead was in contact, who claimed to know the finders, and suggested that material from the site spanned the period from the early Bronze Age (*c.* 2200–1700 BC) to the Iron Age (*c.* 700 BC–AD 43), and that it had been discovered in the Salisbury area. But no real breakthrough came until four years later, when a journalist put one of the actual finders in contact with Ian Stead. This man, who would only call himself John, said that he had a number of finds in addition to photographs of all the artefacts found in the deposit. He wanted to sell his finds for £20,000 and, as part of the deal, said he would inform the buyer of the provenance. A meeting was consequently set up in the Red Lion pub in Salisbury so that the finds could be viewed by Dr Stead who John was now hoping would become the purchaser on behalf of the British Museum.

Dr Stead continued to investigate the case over the following months, whilst keeping in contact with the mystery John. During September 1993, Dr Stead discovered the real identity of John, unbeknown to him, and his accomplice. As the British Museum was not forthcoming with the fee that he wanted, John decided to reduce his price from £20,000 to £10,000 in the hope that it would encourage the Museum to buy from him.

In cases like this, it might seem strange that the police are not involved in the investigation of what are, in effect, stolen goods. But stolen antiquities present the police with enormous difficulties. Not only are they often of low priority in terms of police time, but it is also often very difficult to prove that any crime has been committed. Ancient artefacts are effectively ownerless because the original owners have long since deceased. So, whereas goods stolen from living people can potentially be identified as such and a conviction made, it is virtually impossible to prove that any ancient artefacts have been stolen from a particular site unless the thief is caught red-handed. In the case of the Salisbury hoard, however, Ian Stead was very fortunate to have the help of DCI Jack Woods from Holborn Police. This meant that, after another meeting

111 Searching for the burial pit of the Salisbury hoard, Wiltshire. It was only through the perseverance of Dr Ian Stead that the site of the hoard could be properly investigated.

between Stead and the finder, the police were able to arrest John and his accomplice who were charged with possessing stolen property. By this stage, much of the assemblage had been sold on the antiquities market and divided amongst different dealers, a complex network which Ian Stead was gradually able to trace.

Excavation of the Salisbury hoard site

Although John was not prepared to cooperate, his accomplice agreed to show Dr Stead the findspot of the hoard. With a small team from the British Museum he was thus finally able to excavate the findspot of the Salisbury hoard in 1993 (fig. 111) near the village of Netherhampton. By doing so, the team established that this large assemblage of metalwork had been deposited in a pit, probably originally associated with an Iron Age settlement, such as a farmstead, which had been abandoned. Most importantly, because they were able to find additional pieces of metal from the find, it was possible to convict the finders for theft, as they did not have permission to be on the land on which the discovery had been made.[8]

Original rumours of the size of the hoard also appeared to be grossly exaggerated. It seems to have consisted of about 600 objects in total, ranging in date from about 2400–200 BC.[9] This is a huge timespan for a hoard of metalwork, which usually only spans 200 years at most, making this find extremely unusual. The range of material in the assemblage is also very interesting: aside from the miniature shields, there are Bronze Age tools including a large number of socketed axes as well as chisels, gouges, daggers and spearheads (fig. 112). Of Iron Age date, there are a number of miniature cauldrons and another miniature object type in the shape of a 'moustache'. All these miniatures are curious finds as they are small-scale models of larger arms and domestic items used in Iron Age Britain. But, unlike the miniatures of the late medieval period (see p. 118), which were probably used as toys, the Iron Age equivalents are usually thought to have been made for votive reasons. Miniature shields may have been made as offerings to the gods in order to bring good luck in warfare, whilst the cauldron, having obvious associations with food, might perhaps have been associated with a good harvest. So the deposit of this material on Salisbury Plain was probably a ritual act. Even more intriguing are the Bronze Age artefacts which must have been deposited hundreds of years after they were originally made. Ian Stead believes that the only way to account for this is to suggest that the Bronze Age tools and weapons had been discovered in the Iron Age – hoards of such metalwork are relatively common – and reburied in about 200 BC.

112 Some bronze artefacts from the Salisbury hoard, including a miniature shield (bottom right).

Our precious past

Each of the cases outlined in this chapter is an example of the mistreatment of archaeological discoveries by some, and the salvaging of those discoveries by others. As always, in the final analysis, it comes down to different views about what our heritage can offer. At one end of the scale are those motivated by greed – the heritage equivalent of poachers, stealing antiquities from our soil to convert into cash. The looters of Wanborough Roman temple, the Salisbury hoard and the 'Bowl hoard' from Snettisham all fall into this category. In these cases, their actions led instead – at least for those caught – to criminal records; and even when they managed to sell their illegally excavated finds, they would have received only a fraction of the financial benefit which they might have gained if they had reported their finds correctly. Under the rewards system for treasure, finders who declare discoveries properly will be better off – dealers will never offer finders the full market value, unlike the treasure system (see p. 19). In addition, those who choose not to declare finds properly can only harm their reputations.

At the other end of the scale are those motivated by a desire to understand more about our past. These individuals put the historical value of treasure finds above all other considerations. Finders like Charles Hodder, the discoverer of important finds at Snettisham, fall into this group, as do most of those who found the material discussed in this book. These individuals are also behaving as responsible citizens – indeed, such value is now placed on the importance of good 'citizenship' in modern Britain that it is even being taught in schools. But also into this group fall the archaeologists, curators and find specialists – not all of whom are professional – whose work on the material generated by finders is crucial. Without research into finds, the objects could tell us little about the past.

The work of the Portable Antiquities Scheme is also an important development (see p. 27). The Scheme, which from the end of 2003 will cover the whole of England and Wales, provides a mechanism for finders to voluntarily report all their archaeological discoveries. This is the first time that such a system has been in place, and it is a unique project – no other country in the world has anything like it. In the long term, it is hoped that it will make recording archaeological objects, not just treasure, normal practice for amateur finders.

The Government, too, has a responsibility to act to preserve and protect our heritage, and in recent years it has increasingly recognised how such a policy can benefit British cultural life at all levels. Once again, certain individuals have played a big part in this – Lord Perth to name just one (see p. 20) – and the establishment of the All Party Parliamentary Archaeology Group (APPAG), which has 144 members from all political parties, is another positive step. In addition, in 2002 the Government finally acceded to the UNESCO Convention (see p. 28), and it has also expressed its support for a current Private Member's Bill which proposes to make it a criminal offence to deal in illicit antiquities. Of course, much more could always be done – there are always other issues that are higher on the political agenda than heritage – but nonetheless these are moves in the right direction.

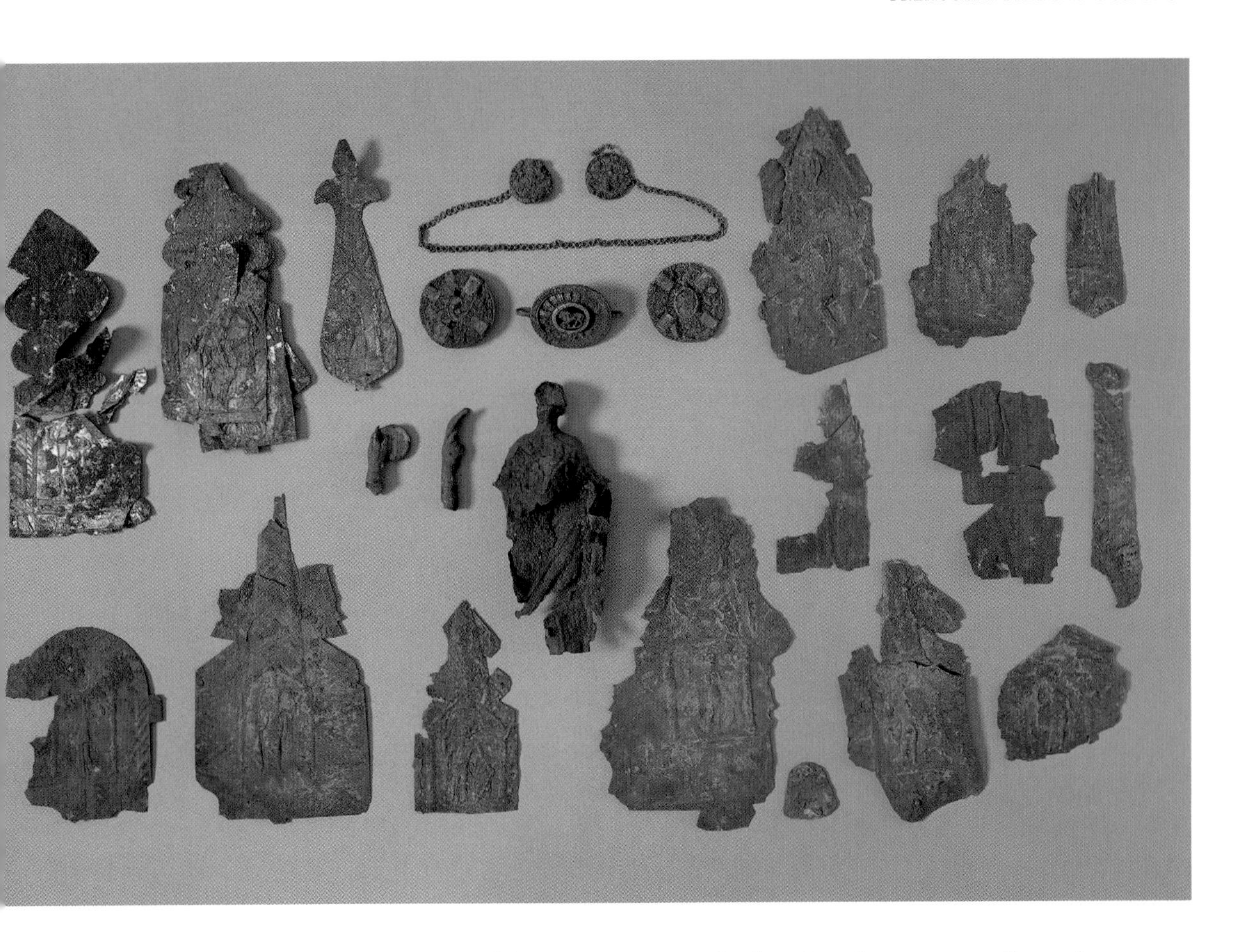

113 New material from a site in Hertfordshire. The discovery of these Roman silver and gold finds demonstrates the dynamic nature of archaeology as new material is constantly coming to light.

Our view of the past is a constantly changing picture as new discoveries come to light. In late 2002, I took a call from a local archaeologist who told me about an extraordinary discovery of Roman silver and gold in Hertfordshire (fig. 113). An arrangement was made for him and the finder to bring the material to the Museum to assess as potential treasure. The site is now being investigated by archaeologists, working alongside the metal detectorist who made the initial discovery, whilst my Museum colleagues are working on the material already found. This discovery, like others before and after, will undoubtedly modify our view of our history, and demonstrates the dynamic nature of archaeology as a subject.

New finds are like additional pieces of a jigsaw of our past and, like all the finds in this book, they illustrate how the discovery of treasure is only the beginning of the story. When we look beyond the glitz and glamour of treasure finds and study them in detail, we may begin to gain a clearer picture of the people that made, used and cherished them. Treasure, like other remains of the past, can offer us an insight into the lives, thoughts and feelings of our ancestors, and show us that they are perhaps not so distant after all.

Advice on reporting archaeological finds

The following advice has been partially reproduced from Hobbs et al. 2002, Appendix 1. For the full version please refer to that publication.

1 Be aware of reporting obligations

Treasure finds must be reported under the 1996 Treasure Act, and other finds can be reported voluntarily with the Portable Antiquities Scheme. For further information please contact:

Outreach Officer
PORTABLE ANTIQUITIES SCHEME
c/o Department of Coins & Medals
British Museum
London WC1B 3DG

Alternatively visit www.finds.org.uk

Finds of wreck (anything that is found in or on the sea, or washed ashore from tidal water) should be reported to:
THE RECEIVER OF WRECK
Spring Place
105 Commercial Road
Southampton SO15 1EG

2 Join a national representative body

Metal detectorists are strongly advised to become members of bodies which represent their interests. Further details can be obtained from the following two organisations:

NATIONAL COUNCIL
FOR METAL DETECTING (NCMD)
Contact: The Secretary
51 Hill Top Gardens
Denaby
Doncaster DN12 4SA
Website: www.ncmd.co.uk

FEDERATION OF INDEPENDENT
DETECTORISTS (FID)
Contact: Detector Lodge
44 Heol Dulais
Birchgrove
Swansea
West Glamorgan SA7 9LT
Website: www.newbury.net/fid

3 Always obtain landowner's permission before metal detecting

It is strongly advised that all permission to metal detect on private land is obtained in writing. Common land such as parks and beaches are also likely to be governed by local council bye-laws which will vary over the country. Councils should therefore be contacted for advice.

Metal detecting or any other digging should never be conducted on Scheduled Ancient Monuments (SAMs). For more information on SAMs contact:

ENGLISH HERITAGE
23 Savile Row
London W1X 1AB
Tel.: 0207 973 3000
Website: www.english-heritage.org.uk

4 Ensure that there is agreement regarding ownership of finds

This is particularly important if any finds of treasure are made. Most detectorists agree that any rewards resulting from treasure finds are split equally with the landowner.

5 Only detect on disturbed ploughland and not deeper than plough depth

It is preferable that metal detecting takes place on disturbed ploughland rather than areas of pasture. All finds of both treasure and non-treasure should be reported (see above). If extensive archaeological remains or large assemblages of archaeological material (for example, coin hoards) are discovered, finders are strongly advised to keep the site from further disturbance and seek professional advice.

Notes

CHAPTER 1

1 Department for Culture, Media & Sport, *Treasure Annual Report* 2000, 8.

2 Beard & Coates 1933, 8.

3 *Calendar of Patent Rolls*, Henry IV, 1399–1401 (London 1903), 259.

4 Beard & Coates, *loc. cit.*

5 *Parochial History of Cornwall*, vol. IV, 33.

6 Text supplied by Edward Besly, Department of Archaeology and Numismatics, National Museums & Galleries of Wales.

7 Information supplied by Roger Bland, British Museum.

8 Evans 1864.

9 Information supplied by Catherine Johns.

10 Bland 1996, 13.

11 Evans 1986.

12 Henry de Bracton, *de legibus et consuetudinibus Angliae* (taken from Hill 1936, 191–3, with references).

13 Dobinson & Denison 1995.

14 Gregory 1991.

15 It was also displayed prior to this in spring 2000, as part of the 'Paid in Burnt Silver' temporary exhibition in Room 69a.

16 Department for Culture, Media & Sport, *Treasure Annual Report* 1998–9, 75–6.

17 *Renaissance in the Regions: a New Vision for England's Museums.* Resource 2001.

18 In full, the 1970 United Nations Educational, Scientific and Cultural Organisation (UNESCO) Convention on the Means of Prohibiting and Preventing the Illicit Import, Export and Transfer of Ownership of Cultural Property gives members the right to recover stolen antiquities – primarily ancient and religious artefacts – which surface in the countries of fellow signatories.

19 www.mcga.gov.uk/row.

CHAPTER 2

1 Also the title of a book by Robinson & Aston (2002).

2 Purkiss 2000, 124–6.

3 Joliffe 1948.

4 Reece 2002, 47.

5 'Illis diebus [about 17 March] juxta Wroccestre in loco quidem Bilebury per quendam incantorem Diabolus coactus cuidam puero apparuit; & urnas & navem & domum cum immense auro ostendit.' *Annales Ecclesiae Wigorniensis* (*Annals of Worcester*), XVI. Cal. April (1288).

6 Thomas Wright's *Uriconium* (1872), 330–32.

7 *Diary of Abraham dela Pryne*, 220, under 10 November 1699 (Surtees Society).

8 Anonymous 1972.

9 Randsborg 1980, 45.

10 Latham & Matthews (eds) 1974, 262.

11 Beard & Coates 1933, 74–5.

12 Latham & Matthews (eds) 1974, 280.

13 Kent 1988, 205–6.

14 From a document (D/DGd, M63) in the Essex Record Office, published in translation in *The Evesdropper*, Newsletter of the Suffolk Historic Buildings Group no. 22 (Autumn 2002).

15 Department for Culture, Media & Sport, *Treasure Annual Report* 1994–5, no. 21.

16 Robertson 2001, no. 1618.

17 Hobbs 1997, 64.

18 As reported in the *Guardian*, 4 May 2002.

19 Cadbury 2000.

20 Pryor 2002.

21 Darvill & Fulton 1998.

22 Department for Culture, Media & Sport, *Treasure Annual Report* 2000.

CHAPTER 3

1 The information concerning this find was gathered from a number of sources, including the Wessex Archaeology website (www.wessexarch.co.uk) and their own press releases. Additional information was taken from the report for the Coroner's inquest prepared by Dr Stuart Needham (British Museum) and Andrew Fitzpatrick (Wessex Archaeology). Additional information was also taken from a BBC 2 documentary *Meet the Ancestors* broadcast on 19 February 2003.

2 Ashbee 1978.

3 James 1999.

4 Dio's *Roman History*, LXII, 2: 'around her neck was a large golden necklace'.

5 Although Cunobelin's coins have been found previously in the Midlands, for example in the Silsden hoard, Yorkshire.

6 Besly & Bland 1983.

7 Robertson 2001; *Coin Hoards from Roman Britain*, vols I–XI; Abdy 2002.

8 Dahl 1999.

9 This emerged during an interview with Sydney Holder, Ford's grandson, broadcast by the BBC on New Years Day, 2003, in the programme *Our Top Ten Treasures.*

10 Brailsford 1947.

11 Painter 1977.

12 The diners are Queen Dido and Aeneas, with the third either a Trojan guest at the banquet or Ascanius.

13 Keepax & Robson 1978.

14 Bland & Johns 1993.

15 Guest forthcoming; Johns forthcoming.

16 Department for Culture, Media & Sport, *Treasure Annual Report* 1998–9, no. 63.

17 *Ibid.*, no. 57.

18 Lives of saints often describe them as having humble origins – such as slavery – in order to emphasise their humility. So in the case of Baldehildis, this should not be viewed as historical fact (Leslie Webster, pers. comm.).

19 Department for Culture, Media & Sport, *Treasure Annual Report* 1998–9, no. 177.

20 Department for Culture, Media & Sport, *Treasure Annual Report* 2000, no. 155.

21 *Ibid.*, no. 59.

22 For an introduction to this subject, see Besly 1987.

23 Besly 1998a; 1998b.

24 Edward Besly, pers. comm.

25 Thornton & Cowell 1996.

CHAPTER 4

1 Deetz 1996, 259–60.

2 Based upon information provided by John Davies, Norwich Castle Museum.

3 Information kindly supplied by Elizabeth Walker, National Museums & Galleries of Wales.

4 Varndell 2001.

5 Colin McEwan, Department of Ethnography, British Museum, pers. comm.

6 Cahill 2001.

7 Information supplied by Paul Craddock, Nigel Meeks and Stuart Needham, Department of Conservation and Scientific Research, British Museum. See Meeks, Craddock & Needham forthcoming.

8 Although there is evidence that razors were used in the late Bronze Age.

9 Hill 1997.

10 However a medical use should not be assumed unless such items are found in an archaeological context alongside definite medical tools (Jackson 2002).

11 Jackson forthcoming.

12 Jackson 1993.

13 Caesar, *De Bello Gallico*, V, 14.

14 The only exception to this is a discovery in a cemetery at Thérouanne, France, but this in any case is probably British in origin, either acquired through trade, or more likely because the person buried with the cosmetic set came from Britain (Jackson & Thuillier 1999).

15 Jackson 1985, 171.

16 Crummy & Eckardt forthcoming.

17 Jundi & Hill 1998.

18 Margeson 1997.

19 Leahy & Paterson 2001.

20 Redknap 2000.

21 Graham-Campbell 1992.

22 Forsyth forthcoming; see also Egan 1996.

23 Gaimster *et al.* 2002, 174; some new finds are to be published shortly (Mitchell & Thornton forthcoming).

24 Ward *et al.* 1981, 146.

25 *Ibid.*, 89.

26 A heraldic term for walking left.

27 Johns 1996, 37.

28 Ward *et al.* 1981, 142–3.

29 Description of Mr Wemmick in *Great Expectations* by Charles Dickens (first published 1861).

CHAPTER 5

1 Renfrew 2000, 9.

2 Stead 1998, 147–8.

3 David Bird 1984 (in O'Connell & Bird 1994, 7).

4 Philip de Jersey, Celtic Coin Index, University of Oxford, pers. comm.

5 David Graham, Surrey Archaeological Society, pers. comm.

6 O'Connell & Bird 1994.

7 Stead 1998.

8 The finders received suspended sentences.

9 Stead 1998, 118.

Bibliography

Abdy, R.A. 2002. *Romano-British Coin Hoards.* Shire Publications Ltd, Buckinghamshire.

Anonymous 1972. *Britain's Buried Treasures.* Drive Publications Ltd, London.

Ashbee, P. 1978. 'Amesbury barrow 51: excavations 1960', *Wiltshire Archaeological Magazine* 70/71 (1975/6), 1–60.

Beard, C.R. & Coates, R.A. 1933. *The Romance of Treasure Trove.* Sampson Low Marston & Co. Ltd, London.

Besly, E. 1987. *English Civil War Coin Hoards.* British Museum Occasional Paper 51.

Besly, E. 1998a. 'Welsh treasure from the English Civil War', *Minerva* 9 (4), August edn, 49–51.

Besly, E. 1998b. 'A Civil War hoard from Tregwynt, Pembrokeshire', *British Numismatic Journal* 68, 119–36.

Besly, E. & Bland, R. 1983. *The Cunetio Treasure.* British Museum Press, London.

Bland, R. 1996. 'Treasure Trove and the case for reform', *Art Antiquity and Law* vol. I, 1: 11–26.

Bland, R. & Johns, C.M. 1993. *The Hoxne Treasure: an Illustrated Introduction.* British Museum Press, London.

Brailsford, J.W. 1947 (repr. 1964). *The Mildenhall Treasure.* British Museum Press, London.

Cadbury, D. 2000. *The Dinosaur Hunters: a Story of Scientific Rivalry and the Discovery of the Prehistoric World.* Fourth Estate, London.

Cahill, M. 2001. 'Unspooling the mystery', *Archaeology Ireland*, Autumn edn, 8–15.

Coin Hoards from Roman Britain, vols I–XI.

Crummy, N. & Eckardt, H. forthcoming. 'Regional identities and technologies of the self: nail cleaners in Roman Britain'.

Dahl, R. (illustrated by Ralph Steadman) 1999. *The Mildenhall Treasure.* Jonathan Cape, London.

Darvill, T. & Fulton, A. 1998. *MARS: The Monuments at Risk Survey of England, 1995: Main Report.* Bournemouth and London.

Deetz, P. 1996 (rev. edn). *In Small Things Forgotten: the Archaeology of Early American Life.* Anchor Books, New York.

Dobinson, C. & Denison, S. 1995. *Metal detecting and archaeology in England.* Council for British Archaeology and English Heritage.

Egan, G. 1996. *Playthings from the Past: Toys from the A.G. Pilson Collection* c. *1300–1800.* Jonathan Horne, London.

Evans, A.C. 1986. *The Sutton Hoo Ship Burial.* British Museum Press, London.

Evans, J. 1864. *The Coins of the Ancient Britons.* J. Russell Smith, London.

Forsyth, H. (with contributions by Egan, G., Wang, M. & Griffiths, A.) forthcoming. *Toys, Trifles and Trinkets: Base Metal Miniatures from London,* c. *1350–1750.* Unicorn Press, London.

Gaimster, D., Hayward, M., Mitchell, D. & Parker, K. 2002. 'Tudor silver-gilt dress-hooks: a new class of treasure find in England', *Antiquaries Journal* 82, 157–96.

Graham-Campbell, J. (ed.) 1992. *Viking Treasure from the North West: the Cuerdale Hoard in its Context.* Selected papers from the 'Vikings of the Irish Sea' conference, 18–20 May 1990. Liverpool, National Museums and Galleries on Merseyside, Occasional Paper 5.

Gregory, A. 1991. *Excavations in Thetford, 1980–82, Fison Way. Volume 1.* East Anglian Archaeology Report 53.

Guest, P. forthcoming. *The Late Roman Gold and Silver Coins from the Hoxne Treasure.* British Museum Press, London.

Hill, G. 1936. *Treasure Trove in Law and Practice from the Earliest Time to the Present Day.* Oxford University Press, Oxford.

Hill, J.D. 1997. '"The end of one kind of body and the beginning of another kind of body?" Toilet instruments and "Romanization" in southern England during the first century AD', in Gwilt, A. & Haselgrove, C. (eds), *Reconstructing Iron Age Societies.* Oxbow Monograph 71, Oxford, 96–107.

Hobbs, R. 1997. 'The Mildenhall treasure: Roald Dahl's ultimate tale of the unexpected?', *Antiquity* 71, no. 271, 63–73.

Hobbs, R., Honeycombe, C. & Watkins, S. 2002. *A Guide to Conservation for Metal Detectorists.* Tempus, Gloucestershire.

Jackson, R.P.J. 1985. 'Cosmetic sets from late Iron Age and Roman Britain', *Britannia* 16, 165–92.

Jackson, R.P.J. 1993. 'The function and manufacture of Romano-British cosmetic grinders: two important new finds', *Antiquaries Journal* 73, 165–9.

Jackson, R.P.J. 2002. 'Roman surgery: the evidence of the instruments', in Arnott, R. (ed.), *The Archaeology of Medicine. Papers given at a Session of the Annual Conference of the Theoretical Archaeology Group held at the University of Birmingham on 20 December 1998.* BAR International Series 1046, Oxford.

Jackson, R.P.J. forthcoming. *Cosmetic Grinders: an Illustrated Catalogue and Discussion of a Type Unique to Iron Age and Roman Britain.* British Museum Occasional Paper 104.

Jackson, R.P.J. & Thuillier, F. 1999. 'A British cosmetic set (nécessaire à fard) from Thérouanne (Pas-de-Calais, France)', *Instrumentum* 9, June 1999, 23–4.

James, S. 1999. *The Atlantic Celts: Ancient People or Modern Invention?* British Museum Press, London.

Johns, C.M. 1996. *The Jewellery of Roman Britain.* British Museum Press, London.

Johns, C.M. forthcoming. *The Late Roman Gold and Silver Jewellery and Silver Plate from the Hoxne Treasure.* British Museum Press, London.

Joliffe, J.E.A. 1948. 'The chamber and the castle treasuries under King John', in Hunt, R.W., Pantin, W.A. & Southern, R.W. (eds), *Studies in Medieval History Presented to F.M. Powicke.* Oxford University Press, Oxford.

Jundi, S. & Hill, J.D. 1998. 'Brooches and identities in first century AD Britain: more than meets the eye?', in Forty, C., Hawthorne, J. & Witcher, R. (eds), *TRAC 1997: Proceedings of the Theoretical Roman Archaeology Conference,* 125–37. Oxbow Books, Oxford.

Keepax, C. & Robson, M. 1978. 'Conservation and associated examination of a Roman chest: evidence for woodworking techniques', *The Conservator* 2, 35–40.

Kent, J.P.C. 1988. 'Interpreting coin finds', in Casey, J. & Reece, R. (eds), *Coins and the Archaeologist.* Seaby, London, 201–17.

Latham, R. & Matthews, W. (eds) 1974. *The Diary of Samuel Pepys,* vol. VIII, 1667. G. Bell & Sons Ltd, London.

Leahy, K. & Paterson, C. 2001. 'A new light on Viking presence in Lincolnshire: the artefactual evidence', in Graham-Campbell, J., Hall, R., Jesch, J. & Parsons, D.N. (eds), *Vikings and the Danelaw: Selected Papers from the Thirteenth Viking Congress,* 183–201. Oxbow Books, Oxford.

Margeson, S. 1997. *The Vikings in Norfolk.* Norfolk Museums Service.

Meeks, N.D., Craddock, P.T., and Needham, S.P. forthcoming. 'Bronze Age penannular gold rings from the British Isles: technology and composition', in Rudoe, J. (ed.), *Jewellery Studies, Journal of the Society of Jewellery Historians.*

Mitchell, O. & Thornton, D. forthcoming. 'Three Tudor silver dress hooks', *Antiquaries Journal.*

O'Connell, M.G. & Bird, J., with Cheesman, C. 1994. 'The Roman temple at Wanborough, excavation 1985–86', *Surrey Archaeological Collections* 82, 1–168.

Painter, K.S. 1977. *The Mildenhall Treasure.* British Museum Press, London.

Pryor, F. 2002. *Seahenge: a Quest for Life and Death in Bronze Age Britain.* HarperCollins, London.

Purkiss, D. 2000. *Troublesome Things: a History of Fairies and Fairy Stories.* Penguin, London.

Randsborg, K. 1980. *The Viking Age in Denmark: the Formation of a State.* Duckworth, London.

Redknap, M. 2000. *Vikings in Wales: an Archaeological Quest.* National Museums & Galleries of Wales, Cardiff.

Reece, R. 2002. *The Coinage of Roman Britain.* Tempus, Gloucestershire.

Renfrew, C. 2000. *Loot, Legitimacy and Ownership.* Duckworth, London.

Robertson, A.S., edited by Hobbs, R. & Buttrey, T.V. 2001. *An Inventory of Romano-British Coin Hoards.* Royal Numismatic Society Special Publications 20, London.

Robinson, T. & Acton, M. 2002. *Archaeology is Rubbish.* Channel Four Publications, London.

Stead, I.M. 1991. 'The Snettisham treasure: excavations in 1990', *Antiquity* 65, 447–65.

Stead, I.M. 1998. *The Salisbury Hoard.* Tempus, Gloucestershire.

Thornton, D. & Cowell, M. 1996. 'The "Armada Service": a set of late Tudor dining silver', *Antiquaries Journal* 76, 153–80.

Varndell, G. 2001. 'Ringing the changes: when terminology matters', *Antiquity* 75, 515–16.

Ward, A., Cherry, J., Gere, C. and Cartlidge, B. 1981. *The Ring: from Antiquity to the Twentieth Century.* Thames & Hudson, London.

Illustration acknowledgements

Ashmolean Museum, Oxford, fig. 95

Roger Bland, fig. 49

British Museum, London, figs 1–4, 6, 8, 17–19, 20 (illustration by Karen Hughes), 23, 26, 31, 33 (illustration by Karen Hughes), 36–41, 43, 45–6, 51–2, 54–5, 59–60, 62–4, 66–7, 73, 75–80, 86, 94, 96, 98–106, 108, 111, 113

Michael Busselle, pp. 2–3 (background photograph of field in Wiltshire)

Canterbury Archaeological Trust, figs 27–8

Capitoline Museum © 1990, photo Scala, Florence, fig. 32

Brian Cavill, fig. 112

Richard Hobbs, figs 9–11, 21, 56, 58

Sydney Holder, fig. 44

Ralph Jackson, fig. 16 (outside church)

Catherine Johns, figs 50, 53

Sam Moorhead, fig. 42

Museum of London, figs 87–93

National Museum of Ireland, fig. 74 (painting by Ursula Mattenberger)

National Museums & Galleries of Wales, figs 7, 15, 65, 69–72, 82–5, 97

Norfolk Museums and Archaeology Service, figs 61, 68

Portable Antiquities Scheme, figs 5, 12–14, 22, 29–30, 81 (drawing by Marina Elwes)

Suffolk County Council Archaeological Service, figs 47, 57

Surrey Archaeological Society, figs 107, 109–10

University of Leicester Archaeological Services, figs 34–5

Vatican Museums, fig. 48

Wessex Archaeology, figs 24, 25 (painting copyright Jane Brayne)

Index